PEOPLE DON'T KNOW
WHAT THEY DON'T KNOW

RICH SMITH

Copyright © 2021 Rich Smith.

All rights reserved. No part of this book may be reproduced, stored, or transmitted by any means—whether auditory, graphic, mechanical, or electronic—without written permission of both publisher and author, except in the case of brief excerpts used in critical articles and reviews. Unauthorized reproduction of any part of this work is illegal and is punishable by law.

Scripture quotations marked NASB are taken from The New American Standard Bible®, Copyright © 1960, 1962, 1963, 1968, 1971, 1972, 1973, 1975, 1977, 1995 by The Lockman Foundation. Used by permission.

ISBN: 978-1-948928-29-8 (sc)
ISBN: 978-1-948928-35-9 (hc)
ISBN: 978-1-948928-38-0 (e)

Because of the dynamic nature of the Internet, any web addresses or links contained in this book may have changed since publication and may no longer be valid. The views expressed in this work are solely those of the author and do not necessarily reflect the views of the publisher, and the publisher hereby disclaims any responsibility for them.

CONTENTS

Dedication v

Preface vii

Chapter 1   My Testimony 1

Chapter 2   Know Who You Are in Christ 10

Chapter 3   Effective Prayers 21

Chapter 4   Articles Written About the World Versus Jesus 32

Chapter 5   More of the Bible Revealed 48

Chapter 6   Keys To Healing 66

Chapter 7   Mike Brawan's Word From God 70

Conclusion 75

DEDICATION

This book is dedicated to all those people that seek for and are learning to live by the ABSOLUTE TRUTH, which is Jesus. Also, I want to dedicate this book to all the people who inspired me to go to Kenya to be a missionary. There are too many to name, but included is Pastor Mike Brawan in Kenya and from the Jubilee International Church in Pensacola, Florida, with Pastor Len Ballenger. This book was suggested by Pastor Mike Brawan of the Metro International Church while I was in Nakuru, Kenya, and his inspiration was and still is beyond what I can write. And I want to mention his church staff that are dedicated and very successful to help make Metro Church ministry the most "known" church in Kenya with the Grace of God.

PREFACE

I have been writing articles for years about the topic, "People don't know what they don't know." And too many don't know that they don't know, because they think they know everything THEY need to know, especially about Jesus, whether they have accepted Him or not. Then there are those who DON'T want to know, because they fear it would interfere with their lifestyle one way or the other. Also, understand that "to know" in the Bible is an intimate relationship. And after a period of time of the process of getting to know Jesus through belief, because of the interrelationship with the Holy Spirit, you go from believing to "knowing" it all as fact! This is really critical in these "end days" (more later), of how to still be blessed in the midst of this "new government."

Hence, the other reason to republish, is because, due to the "process" of the election for the President of the USA, our country is presumably now in the hands of a people who mostly don't really KNOW Jesus as per their platform of supporting abortion and sex perversion, among many other unrighteous things. But as per Exodus 14:14, where Moses is about to take the people across the Red Sea, he said, "Hold your peace", and after they crossed, all the armies (forces against righteousness) were destroyed. Wait upon the Lord.....and see, whether it is sooner or later. He still has a special purpose for this country.

So this book will greatly help those of us that understand or grow to understand how to keep Jesus first as we contend with the "things" to come. But I pray that many will read this book, or similar ones, so that they would get on the side of righteousness with Jesus.

I accepted Jesus in 1981, and had the immediate desire to "want to know what I didn't know" about Him. More to come later of the process I went through and still do. So this book's main purpose is for you to get to really KNOW Jesus. Most of this information is fairly simple, and for many, it will remind them of some things they have forgotten. Example, there have been discussions for years about whether Jesus is black or white or whatever. Folks, He's Jewish! Now, if you are new at being a Christian, this book should be ideal for you. Included will be material that is very little or not covered at all by many denominations or religions. Some of the reasons will be obvious to Full Gospel experienced men and women of God. Much of the book is based on my own experiences and how the Word gave me the appropriate information to know God's Point of view, although I was not always perfect at it. This is my first book and there is very little use of big words to try to impress you. Let's just use the K.I.S.S. principle: Keep It Simple (you fill in the last 'S').

So the end result, I pray, is for those that read this, that it will reinforce what you already know, but maybe with another way to SEE it. Also, for many you will find out the critical value and a higher level of wisdom than before, of what you didn't know before that you NOW know, leading to the wisdom "to still seek what you still don't know", after this book. I will add here an example that, yes, I am still learning. I have basically finished this book, but I am including this that I learned this morning from my pastor here in Kenya. Yes, I knew that we should put God first in everything. Then he mentioned Genesis 1:1, the first verse: "In the beginning God….." God is the same yesterday, today, and tomorrow. He wants all mankind to 'keep' Him in our 'beginning' of everyday and everything we do…… the first thing He writes for us to KNOW. Then he put that together with John 1:1, "In the BEGINNING was the Word, and the Word was with God, and the Word was God."(caps mine). The "Word" is Jesus (see verse 14). So Jesus IS the 'beginning,' and so is the Holy Spirit (Genesis 1:2). What a revelation! Keep this in mine as you read this book, but also in everything you do about putting God first in your life. He IS the beginning!

Also, KNOW that in these last days (more on this later), we, in Christ, will come under persecution, maybe from several directions. But the more you KNOW Jesus, this is not a major problem, because you will have or be gaining the 'boldness of using' the Authority of the Name of Jesus to make a stand against and thwart your persecutors. Don't be confused, because, as with me, we have the joy of the rest of eternity with God of discovering many more "things to know". But note this now: I pray you have now, or will develop as you read, the seriousness, for the sake of your blessings here on earth, and fulfilling God's purpose for your life, that you will develop the steadfast passion for it, to even become a habit, despite life's challenges (trust God's help all along the way, Psalms 91: 15 & 16) of discovering "what you didn't know that you now know" is far above what you can even imagine now.

My methods through the almost 40 years of seeking to know Jesus has, been through daily prayers, but not just to pray, but to decree His Word for my life. I also have read the Bible several times, and I read many books from mighty men and women of God (if you seek God seriously, He will lead you to the right sources). I gave away 80 books to a jail ministry a while back and still had over a hundred left. Also, over the years I have constantly listened to CD's from many of those same authors. Every time I drove somewhere in my car I would listen to the CD's including 42 on the book of Revelation and 19 on the book of Daniel, all listened to many times. I also took notes in the churches where there was information that I either did not know or it was a different look at material I was familiar with. Another process I went through is to DO the righteous things that "came to my mind" as time went on. I also watched several Christian TV broadcasts many times. This was all done along with the rest of life of "making a living and raising a family."

Some of those men and women of God: Kenneth and Gloria Copeland, Dr. Mike Evans from the Jerusalem Prayer team, Joel Rosenberg from the Joshua Fund ministry, Billye Brim, Sid Roth, Creflo Dollar, Kynan Bridges, Dr. David Jeremiah, Hal Lindsey, and so many others since 1981. Also, my main bible reference is the NKJV, copyright 1983 by Thomas Nelson, Inc. And many of those verses will be paraphrased, and the parenthesis are mine. Realize, also, there is no gender; "man" is both male and female unless specifically written. To God be the glory for all the benefits this book brings you as well as me.

CHAPTER 1

MY TESTIMONY

When I wrote this book, I was a full time missionary in Kenya, Africa, from February, 2020 to October, 2020. I am also an ordained pastor in Nakuru, Kenya, working with a mighty man of God, Dr. Reverend Mike Brawan, who is well known in all of Kenya with the people and government. He is well known also in many other countries and many states in the USA, as he has been a featured speaker many times in so many places.

I was born in 1948, one and a half months before Israel became a nation. I am from the Pensacola, Florida area. When I was 14, we moved to Arizona for my dad's health. I finished high school there and immediately joined the US Air Force in 1966 at the age of 18. My first assignment was in the Philippines where I met and married a Filipina when I was 19. She had a daughter 2 years old. I helped raise her as my daughter, and I now have 3 grandchildren and 3 great grandchildren, with another on the way due in May, 2021, through her. Boy, did I start young with a family! My wife was Roman Catholic, and I had not committed to anything yet, but at the time I thought it was at least something. See I had pretty much believed in Jesus most of my life up to then, but was too shy to go to the altar to accept Him. But after a while of attending masses I became discouraged with the Catholic "way", as it seemed too ritualistic TO ME, and I was not learning anything from the very short "sermons". So life went on.

I went to the war in Vietnam in 1970, still being a non-Christian. I was in construction and repair there. But one Saturday morning about 1:00 AM, our base came under attack with incoming rockets. They kept coming in about every 5 minutes the rest of the night. The sound of each rocket was like the loudest CLAP of thunder you have ever heard, and each one shook my "hut" with dust falling everywhere. So I met, in my mind, the real MR. FEAR! I was under my bed expecting at any time one of those rockets to land on me. Yes, I prayed. Well, the next morning I found that it was NOT an attack. Our ammo dump had been sabotaged by the enemy, and each "rocket" was actually a stack of bombs exploding. But under my bed, I did not know that, so my fear was real to me. So life went on going to different bases in the Air Force and still raising my family. We birth 2 boys, one in 1968 and the other in 1973.

In 1973, I qualified to be sent to a university in Arizona to get a degree in Civil Engineering to become an officer afterwards. The Air Force paid all expenses, including moving my family and household there. In 1976 after graduation I went for the "90 days" in Officer Training School to become a Lieutenant. Then more assignments, more traveling, still raising the family.

At one of those assignments near Pensacola, Florida, in 1981, in my spare time, I started a business of my own. The group I was working with were Christians, and every 3 months we would have a weekend function where on Sunday mornings we would have non-denomination Christian services. That same year my wife and I went to accept Jesus at one of those weekend services.

Immediately, I started on the journey of "wanting to know Jesus and His Word". I began reading the Bible, and many other books. It was actually that business that instilled in me to make a habit of daily reading and listening to tapes. I also started daily prayers and taking notes in churches of various denominations. I have volumes of those notes stockpiled. I still take notes if it is something new or another way of expressing something I already knew. I watched a lot of Christian TV, too, all that to get to know Jesus, and His purpose for me. I even went to some Catholic masses occasionally to keep my wife happy, although she did not take up the journey of "wanting to know" as I did. So, believe me, it caused a LOT of conflicts. My love for her was for her to learn the value, as God has in His Word, for the "two to become one" (Matt 19:5). She never really fully adapted, but I kept growing, but not being perfect to handle it all. I even had flesh problems of anger and sexual desires. But, amongst the many truths of God I was learning and trying to adapt into my lifestyle, I learned the verse, 1 John 1:9, "If you confess your sins, He is ready to forgive you", and you just carry on with God. So life went on.

I retired as an Air Force captain in 1986. I did several jobs in management and selling. Then in 2002, I started driving the big trucks, 18 wheelers. I drove nationwide awhile and then some local jobs with different companies. Then in 2006 I volunteered to go to the war in Iraq as a convoy truck driver under a military contract 35 years after leaving the war in Vietnam. How many people do you know has been in 2 wars, 35 YEARS APART? I went to make better money, but I still pursued getting to KNOW Jesus. I met a teacher of pastors who taught me a lot that I still use today. He also advised to start focusing on Israel, God's chosen people (realize as a child of God you are adopted Jews under the heir of Abraham). The epicenter of all the world's events and problems past, present, and future is Israel. That is another major study.

So now in Iraq, I still pursued Jesus in between and during missions while waiting on the pick up or deliveries of materials, supplies, and equipment on our flatbed trailers. Remember I was now a Christian. Before any convoy I was on left a base, amongst other prayers, I always decreed, "No weapon formed or fashioned against me (or this convoy, I would add) shall prosper." (Isaiah 54:17). Know that any convoy on a mission had to leave a protected base. We always had a few Army vehicles with weapons and devices to try to find any IED's (Improvised Explosive Devices) on the road, but we truck drivers were NOT allowed ANY weapons. None of my convoys were ever attacked 19 months in Iraq. There were other convoys that were attacked, and we came close a few times. Many times, though, some of the bases we were on did come under attack by rockets and/or mortars. Throughout all the time I was there, I had many challenges of harsh climate (extreme heat, sand storms, etc.), bad management, truck problems, etc., but I never experienced that man, MR FEAR!

On June of 2008 on my last mission, that had been about a week long, I received a Red Cross message that my wife was in a near death situation. Since we kept our passports with us at all times, I was able to go by helicopter back to Baghdad, where we had just left about an hour earlier, to catch a flight home. She passed while I was there. All my children, some other of mine and her relatives, and some friends were there. After all final arrangements and services I went back to Iraq to turn in all my gear and pack clothes, etc. We had been married 40 years.

So life went on of getting to know Jesus, but with less distractions, but still not being perfect. But I had discovered the more you give of your time and money to Jesus, you gain more wisdom and boldness with HIS Word, and your needs are met. I developed a deep desire to strive to do what Jesus said in John 14:12, "….the works that I do you will do also; and greater works than these you will do…." I put myself as the "you" and knew that "greater works" did not mean better works, but just more, because Jesus only ministered for 3 years. Even when I had a job, I would get up an hour earlier for all my prayers and decrees and seeking Ephesians 1:18, "...what is the hope of His calling for me..." I started driving school bus in 2009 and retired from working at that job in 2015.

After my wife passed I put even more into seeking God's Will for my life. I constantly did righteous things like giving to the church and other ministries. I went to Israel 3 times looking for a ministry that I could actively use my time. But other than donations to those ministries, there were no "positions" available. I also did a lot of jail ministering, with excellent results of salvations.

Then in mid 2017, I was watching one of my Christian TV broadcasts. The guest was the founder of Impact Nations. He said that they train volunteers from around the world to go to many nations per year, training them to be missionaries for healing, feeding, delivering, etc. Just what I had been praying for years to do His works. I was about to sign up for the next trip to Nepal, but I called Impact Nations for a couple questions and the founder's wife answered. After some conversation, she said I should go to Tanzania in Africa, since they would be on that trip, and it was about the same time frame. I signed up immediately for this 2 week trip. But before the trip that Government was having problems, so the trip was changed to Kenya for the same dates. See how God works!

Because this is where I met Pastor/Dr. Mike Brawan of the Metro International Church in Nakuru. He was the on site coordinator for all the missions for the team in many places in Kenya, where we did medical clinics, installed water filters, fed thousands of kids, did hands on healing, visited prisons and the Nakuru dump site where many of the poor lived, and we were guest speakers at several churches (Mike had started over 100 churches in Kenya), and several of the team had gone to rescue prostitutes. Mike has also rescued, along with these women, other women and men from the streets, prisons, and the dump and put thousands over the years into more small businesses like using bicycles and motor bikes as taxi's, tailoring shops, sewing shops, sales jobs, salons, selling food at the side of the road, and more. I have met several and was a customer for some.

While the team of about 25 were traveling by bus to all the places we went, Mike would, tirelessly, be teaching great mysteries in the Word. Because of all the seeking I had done since 1981, I told him that from all my studies, mostly from Kenneth Copeland, he was right on target, and I was still learning from him. A little later the team was gathered in his church for more teaching. Mike called me out of the audience and prophesized over me. That had never happened to me. He then told me that he was my spiritual father, and I had never had a GOOD MENTOR in the Word. Well, hear this: This man was doing the works of Jesus and greater works, what I had been seeking to do for years! Praise God for leading me step by step all those years, because I "did not faint" (Gal 6:9). I have met several mighty men and women of God through Mike. What a blessing.

In early 2018 I went with Impact Nations to Samar, Philippines, that had severe damage from an earlier typhoon (hurricane). Remember my wife was Filipina. In 1997 we had went to live there, because the business, where I had become a Christian in 1981, was being opened there for the first time. This was after I had retired from the military in 1986. We stayed for about 18 months, where I was hired by a millionaire to help him expand the business for his group which I was in. I did a lot of travel, including some ministering throughout the country. What an adventure. So the trip in 2018 was like a homecoming.

Then in October of the same year I went back to Kenya with Impact Nations and stayed over a week longer to be with Pastor Mike. I went again to Kenya by myself July and August of 2019. With constant contact and donations for Mike's ministry all along, we decided towards the end of 2019 for me to sell my house, car, and furniture. Why should I continue with all that debt when I had been called by God to go to Kenya? I put some personal stuff in a small storage unit. So after all that was settled, I moved to Kenya February of 2020 to be a full time missionary and also, I had been ordained as a pastor in Mike's church when I was there in 2019 by a Bishop, a Kenyan, who was part of Mike Brawan's early ministry and establishing churches.

During the time from 2018 and 2019 Mike had come to the USA twice to be a featured speaker in several churches where I was with him at some of those places including Bushnell, Florida, Sioux Falls, South Dakota, Buffalo, New York, Meadville, Pennsylvania, Baton Rouge, Louisiana, and in Newark, New Jersey, and a country place in southern Connecticut. Also, he had stayed with me in my home in Gulf Breeze, Florida, next to Pensacola. When he came there in 2018 he wanted me to take him to Pensacola to meet a friend. The wife was cofounder of the Jubilee International Church with her husband who had passed about 4 years prior to our visit. Due to Mike's influence she is now married to a man who had proposed to her in Mike's church in Nakuru. So since they had close connection to Mike, and more important, this church was very similar to Mike's church, I immediately joined. On Mike's next visit in 2019, he was the featured speaker the Sunday he was there. That church sponsored me in Kenya, and 5 ladies came from there came here right I arrived in February, 2020. At this time a crusade was in progress. Many were delivered, healed, and demons cast out at this crusade. All the places where Mike Brawan was the featured speaker in the USA, I witnessed many delivered, healed, and demons cast out. After that crusade we visited some prisons, the market place, the dump site, schools, and other churches. During all the times I have been in Kenya, there have been several crusades with all the same kind of results.

Right after this crusade ended, the first week of March, the 5 ladies left JUST before the corona virus restrictions started. God's great engineering again on the timing! Yes, the fear it created got all the schools, churches, and many businesses closed there, too, like most of the "world". We came immediately against it by the Authority of the Name of Jesus. We still had to wear the masks, and "pretend" social distancing, and wash our hands, etc. to keep the police away. But even as I wrote this book, as of 10 June, 2020, there had been no deaths and only about 5 reports there in Nakuru with a population of over 2 million. All this time from March to June, the entire Nakuru, especially downtown and in the market place, did NOT practice social distance very good and not all in masks. We discovered and already knew our "enemy" that the whole restrictions worldwide were created by man to control the multitude through fear. Yes "their" virus was real but greatly mismanaged due to fear. But using motor bikes, and a few visitors to the church, going to the dump, and a couple villages, we have still fed thousands from March to when I left Kenya in October.

But, again, with God's great engineering, we had been asked, due to Mike's reputation, to appear on TV several times on the news, and on Christian broadcasts, but a lot more often, and every week, on radio Christian broadcasts, and occasionally more TV. See in Kenya, few have TV's, but all have radios. Also, Mike had been using, even before corona, streaming, through his i-phone to reach a multitude, including all the prisons there and other countries like India, the USA, England, Australia, Canada, and several other countries in Africa. So, praise God, we reached millions more than before corona. And we knew that God is engineering much more after the restrictions are gone. We finally had been allowed to go to some poor villages to minister through feeding, blessing, and healing.

I pray knowing my background and the kind of ministry God led me to, that you will keep reading so you will experience for yourself the rewards of "seeking to know Jesus" all for God's glory, and I am sure for your blessings. It will be mostly teaching through my experiences of how God's wisdom will be vital in your circumstances to come. If you are sincere to yourself to "want to know what you don't know" about Jesus, or you are developing the desire as you read, don't treat my "teachings" as casual or routine. There are so many critical FACTS in God's Word that will provide you what YOU need to receive the answers needed AS they are needed to confront the challenges you WILL face, as we are in the "end days" before Jesus comes. The JOY that will bring is beyond any words that I could write.

CHAPTER 2

KNOW WHO YOU ARE IN CHRIST

Some basic truths: No matter who you are from whatever country, whatever race, religion, gender, rich or poor, worst sinner, or born sinner (as we all are), young (even the unborn and aborted) or old, successful or homeless, with a job or in jail, filled in your belly or starving, healthy or sick, wise or ignorant (people don't know what they don't know), with Jesus or without Jesus, and I am sure I missed someone, but no matter: The ONE and ONLY true living God who is omniscient (all knowing), omnipotent (all powerful), omnipresent (existing simultaneously, past, present, and eternity future), LOVES you no matter your sins. There is the story from a great evangelist that in his prison ministry, he met a man on death row who was convicted of being a serial killer of, I think over 20 women. He was delivered through this evangelist, and they became friends. Before he was executed this man converted everyone else on death row. In the chair to be given the lethal injection, they asked if he had anything to say. He gave all of them a sermon, and just before he went "under" he gave a thumbs up through the window to the evangelist as he watched. That man is with Jesus, because a true Christian or any child below the age of understanding, including the aborted one, "Absent from the body, present with the Lord" (2 Cor 5:8).

So, per the book of Genesis, due to God's love, He created man in His image (this is a huge sermon here) to be like Him. He gave the first man, Adam, dominion of the entire earth. And the only creature, man, he gave FREE WILL. So Adam walked and talked with God. But there was only one law: "Don't eat from the one tree of knowledge of good and evil" (Genesis 2:17). So Satan, that had been banished to earth for his sin of pride (God's worst sin), used that one law to tempt Adam and Eve. They used their FREE WILL to eat of the tree. By breaking that one law, they brought sin into this world and gave dominion of it to Satan. So every human born since then was born with a sin nature. Many years later, this led to so much critical sin that God found only one godly man, Noah and his family, so he destroyed the world with the great flood saving Noah and family and 2 of every animal. The same thing happened later with the destruction of Sodom and Gomorrah. The 2 main sins for both events was the sacrifice of babies and sex perversion. Wow, look how far we have "come" in this world where both are legalized by the USA government and other countries of this "world" where Satan has dominion!

But God already planned that He would send His sinless son, Jesus, to be born of a virgin. Jesus healed, taught and made whole a multitude in His 3 year ministry starting at the age of 30, after receiving the baptism of the Holy Spirit. Romans 6:23 says "the wages of sin is death (this includes all humans born with the sin nature)." But even though still sinless, Jesus was crucified on the cross where God, due to His love of all, put for ALL mankind, every disease of any kind, poverty, sin, and death onto Jesus so it would be taken to hell and given back to Satan. And since Jesus was sinless, illegal in hell, God resurrected Him from hell, the only man of any religion to be raised from the dead. So even though man is still born with the sin nature, He can use his FREE

WILL to accept Jesus, God's ONLY plan of salvation. Jesus said in John 14:6, "I am the Way, the Truth, and the Life. No one comes to the Father except through Me." Also, in this way you get back the same dominion of this world that Adam had. But to fully gain what you now have through Jesus, there is much to come to "know what you don't know" of WHO you are in Christ. When you accept Jesus through belief (check Romans 10:9, that I will cover later), He sends the Holy Spirit to manifest Himself into your spirit. See, know that God is also, the Son, Jesus, and the Holy Spirit. Man is a spirit, who possesses a mind and soul, who lives in the flesh, the body (see 1 Thess 5:23). So even as you automatically receive the Holy Spirit into your spirit, it will take some time, some longer than others, to get the mind and body to catch up with that NEW spirit. This leads to the main purpose of this book: to discover "what you don't know"..........yet. So pretty much the rest of your reading......is that process.

This process is based on Rom 12:2 (parenthesis mine), "Do not be conformed to this world (as a Christian now, you are not part of this world, which I will cover more later), but be transformed (like a caterpillar changes into a butterfly) by the renewing of your mind, that you may prove what is that good and acceptable and perfect will of God." This "renewing" is steady, pretty much daily for better effectiveness, of praying, reading, listening to the Word, taking notes or recording in church, doing the right thing as it comes to your mind, giving your tithes and offerings (trusting God with your finances), etc. All this will be discussed in more detail later.

I discovered the more I stayed steady at all this, the more God gave me, so I could "give" more for His purpose.

YOUR AUTHORITY

John 8:32, "You shall know the truth, and the truth shall set you free. Also, 2 Tim 1:7, "God has not given you the spirit of fear, but of power, love, and a sound mind." Being set free and having a sound mind are very similar. But both are gained over a period of constantly seeking (pretty much daily) to KNOW Jesus. Don't you want that BOLD confidence of the "freedom" of knowing the absolute truth (it's not your truth or mine.....it is the absolute truth) that gives you a sound mind? If you only knew how this is critical in your everyday life......and you WILL, if you don't quit!

This is very significant in "doing the works of Jesus and greater works" (John 14:12). Then in John 16:15 (paraphrased), "All things that the Father has are Mine (Jesus) and that God will take of Mine and declare it to you (we Christians seeking to know Jesus)." Did Jesus heal, cast out demons, raise the dead, feed the multitude, and much more? Join me to desire to do what Jesus wants of us.

Also, again, this process of Romans 12:2, which has been my main focus since 1981, "Do not be conformed to this world (of deception, disease, sin, death, poverty, worry, depression, using credit cards to buy what you can't afford, etc.), but be transformed (like a caterpillar turning into a butterfly) by the renewing (a constant daily action) of your mind (catching up to the truth that your spirit already knew which you received when you accepted Jesus). I still today am renewing my mind daily.

Now in your reading, this is a great time for those that don't know Jesus and have read enough that you want in on this "process" to get to know Jesus. HOW? Romans 10:9 is one way: "That if you confess with your mouth, 'Jesus is Lord', and believe in your heart that God raised Him from the dead, you will be saved." You have to say it with your own mouth so your ears can hear it. This can be done anywhere, including in a church, but once you have confessed it, find a whole Bible believing church teaching from Genesis to Revelation, so you can learn more and associate with fellow believers that will help you "grow in Christ".

So SAY this right where you are now, what I have written, and even some of you may say it to renew vows, "Father God in Heaven, thank you for your Son, Jesus. I am a sinner, I cannot save myself through my works. Jesus, I believe you died for my sins. I believe You rose from the dead. Please forgive me of all my sins. Come into my heart, fill me with Your Holy Spirit, and make me be the person You want me to be. Amen!" Congratulations, and if this is your first time, don't go by what you 'feel', go by your belief that you did Romans 10:9, and you have complied with God's Word. Now "get on with discovering what you don't know"!

Realize that "being saved" is translated to Salvation, total wholeness or "fullness of God", (Ephesians 3:19). When Jesus died on the cross, he died with God putting on Him ALL sin, death, sickness, disease, pestilence, and poverty so He could take it all to Satan and give it all back to him, thus conquering him (we are also conquerors, per Romans 8:37), then He was resurrected, the only man of any religion having done so. This, also, gave us our dominion back that he stole from Adam. God and sin cannot coexist, so this is also, a reminder of why Jesus is the ONLY Way to God to be with Him for eternal life, because as we are all born with the sin nature, accepting Jesus is the only way to rid of that sin. Now getting that dominion back is one of the main objectives to know Jesus, so we will be more effective in our works of His. Per 1 Thessalonians 5:23, we are 3 parts, like God, the Son, and the Holy Spirit. We are a spirit (God 'breathed' it in us at our creation), we possess a mind and a soul, and we live in this shell of a body. After accepting Jesus, He sends His perfect Spirit with the total Truth of being totally healed, containing no poverty, having total deliverance from sin to manifest your spirit. Now this was ALL done before you and I were born.

But the mind and body being 'X' years old are so used to the old way, it will take time, some longer than others, to catch up to the Truth. So how fast do you want to be effective at telling your body that you

ARE healed, and the body RESPONDS? I have been doing this for years, saying "I never get sick", and I am 72 years 'young'! It directly corresponds to the commitment you make to yourself and God to consistently seek to KNOW Jesus. The old phrase, "practice makes perfect", definitely applies here. Are you going to be always preparing for 'whatever' or will you just let 'whatever' prepare you? Accept by saying this decree for yourself, "I have the Authority of the Name of Jesus and…..nothing by any means shall hurt me!" (Luke 10:19)

Some might say, "But I have so many problems, or so many things needed, or I am behind on my bills, etc." So, Matthew 6:33, "But seek first the Kingdom of God and His righteousness and all these things shall be added onto you. Therefore, do not worry about tomorrow for tomorrow will worry about its own things…."

Righteousness is to do what seems to be the right thing to do or say in any given situation. If done with your heart, but didn't work, remember, Romans 8:28 (parenthsis mine), "All things (good or bad) work out together for good for those that love the Lord, and are called to His purpose." Believe me, love grows as you seek and do, and God has a purpose for all His children, and not necessarily becoming a missionary like me.

YOUR TONGUE

I have stressed for years, you have to be careful what you say. Proverbs 6:2 (parenthesis mine), "You are snared (trapped) by the words of your own mouth." You can be "trapped" into a negative life or a life with many blessings. Proverbs 18:21, "Death and life are in the power of the tongue…" Isaiah 50:4, "The Lord God hath given me the tongue of the learned that I should know how to speak….".

The more you practice restraint of a wrong tongue and get to KNOW Jesus, the more you speak FOR Him, the more "learned" you will become of how and what He wants you to speak.

So because of our flesh, our tongue is one of two greatest enemies. The other is pride. I have experienced in my own life with some of my own relatives of how damaging pride can be.

The first sin and God's worst sin is pride, and it is the most violated by mankind. Man has difficulty being humble, a major, major hindrance in getting to know Jesus. Also, Lucifer, the highest of the Angels, was the first with this sin. In Isaiah 14:12-15, he said with his tongue 5 different ways that he "will" be better than God, which is pride at its worst. This got him kicked out of heaven as Satan.

So back to the tongue. I am 72 years "young" as of April, 2020. I have said many times in public, in church, and in writing articles, "I never get sick." I have said, jokingly, "If I see the flu coming, I duck my head." I have not received the flu shot since I retired from the Air Force in 1986, where it was mandatory once a year. Only once in a safety meeting while I was a school bus driver in 2014. But why is this all true? Because I SAY it! Most everyday, even now, in my prayers, I say, "By His stripes, I am healed." (Isaiah 53:5) If I have a headache or whatever trying to come on me I say, "By the Authority of the Name of Jesus, headache (or what ever) be gone!" Again, the more you know Jesus, the more you realize without a doubt "that" authority you have in the Name of Jesus, because IT WORKS! Sometimes it may not go away immediately, but stick to the confessing with your mouth. So the bolder you become not only for yourself, but in the lives of those you encounter.

Remember I am from the Pensacola area in Florida. There have been several times where hurricanes were tracked to hit my area.

After a while of enduring some of these storms, during the process of getting to KNOW Jesus, I reached a point to realize, "this is enough!" So I started decreeing by the Authority of the Name of Jesus, no more damaging storms! Two powerful hurricanes, Katrina and Michael, in different years were tracked to hit our area of Pensacola. So I spoke, "by the AUTHORITY of the Name of Jesus, be gone from here!" Hurricane Katrina was supposed to come up the western coast of Florida and hit Pensacola. But due to my decree, and probably some other Christians, it went straight west then headed for New Orleans. Remember I decreed for it to be gone. After that, it was out of my hands. Some years later, Hurricane Michael, was in the Gulf of Mexico, and had gotten to be the most powerful storm in many years, and it was headed north directly to Pensacola. The day it was supposed to hit I was supposed to fly to a place in the USA to meet with Pastor Mike. So I decreed again for that one to be gone. It suddenly took about a 45 degree turn to the northeast and hit Florida in the least populated area. Some of you have the prerogative to say or think that it was a coincidence, which is a typical response for those that don't know Jesus. Not to be "arrogant", but I was still in Kenya when hurricane Sally hit Pensacola.

Again, boldness comes from knowing who you are in Christ. Reminders:

> Don't speak evil, but speak kindness.
> Don't speak hate, but love.
> Don't speak un-forgiveness, but forgiveness.
> Don't speak of being poor, but of being blessed.
> Don't speak "I can't find a job", but "God has a job waiting on me."
> Don't speak fear of the storm, but for it to be gone.
> Don't speak sickness or disease, but that you are healed.

All this by the Authority of the Name of Jesus. Just remember, that God can't steer a parked car! You have to get out and DO something, especially speaking with the right tongue even after praying.

God created the heavens, the earth, and man with the SPOKEN WORD! He said in Genesis 1:3, "Let there be light; and there was light," as well as the rest of creation. Also, in Isaiah 55:11, "So shall my word be that goes forth from my mouth; It shall not return to Me void, but it shall accomplish what I please, and it shall prosper in the thing for which I sent it." God is the same yesterday, today, and for all eternity. His Word is STILL "prospering" as the way it first went out, even as it is coming out of the mouth of true believers repeating the same Words today! Realize God created you to be like Him. He gave you free will to "choose" to believe or to choose not to believe as with most people, even with many Christians. Example, as I was writing this most of the world was still under the "restrictions" of the corona virus, even though there were very little deaths.….less than the flu!

We in the Metro church had been speaking on national media about allowing the church to have their meetings again. But we discovered that many pastors were resisting, because they "feared" the virus to return!!!

Fear is not of God, therefore it is Unbelief, hence, the wrong choice. The same thing was happening in the USA, and most of the world.….. way too much unbelief, so welcome to a world of turmoil!

But NOT in my house and church. We chose to believe and kicked out the virus right in the beginning. His word did not come back void….no deaths in the over 2 million population of Nakuru. So choose with YOUR free will to believe every Word of God. Romans 15:13, "Now may the God of hope fill you with all joy and peace in believing, that you may abound in hope by the power of the Holy Spirit." Take EACH word of that verse seriously! See 'hope' in the Bible is an assurance that it is coming, so live as if it exists NOW! I remind myself of this 'assurance' with my tongue every day, therefore I am at peace, but with the frustration that I witness most everyday in the world and on TV that the multitude don't LIVE with that same 'assurance', hence, turmoil, and again the purpose of this book.

So God wants the true believer to "speak" His Word so that it does not come back void either, even though sometimes we will not SEE the end results immediately of God's purpose. It may even be after we see the doctor or take medicine. God works through them, too. WHY? Isaiah 55:8, "For My thoughts are not your thoughts, nor are your ways My ways, says the Lord." So just trust our God as His purpose is being done, and you should have peace in that.

In the book, "Authority of the Believer," by John A. MacMillan, (one of the best books, other than the Bible, that I have read) he writes from page 27 to 28, "Do we believe that God 'hath quickened us together, and made us sit together in heavenly places in Christ Jesus?' (Ephesians 2:6). If we do, our reaction to it will be a fervent, 'Lord, I accept Thy gracious word. I believe that Thou hast thus wrought for me. In humble faith I do now take my seat in the heavenly places in Christ Jesus at Thy right hand. Teach me how to fulfill this sacred ministry, how to exercise the authority which Thou hast entrusted to me. Train me day by day that I may attain to the full stature of the perfect man in Christ, so that in me Thy purpose of the ages may be fulfilled'. Amen." I have prayed that since 2016, and still do pray it every day, and I remember each time, "that Thy PURPOSE OF THE AGES may be fulfilled." Hence, for all eternity. And that sincere desire brought me to Kenya as an ordained pastor and missionary endeavoring to "do the works of Jesus, and greater works" for God's glory, not mine! And more from page 27 and 28, "As we continue to abide closely in Him, our prayers for the advancement of the Kingdom will become less and less the uttering of petitions and will increasingly manifest the exercise of a spiritual authority that recognizes no national boundaries, but fearlessly binds the forces of darkness in any part of the world." Remember you have to SPEAK that authority for any situation, good or bad, around the world.

So your health, the status of your finances, your deliverance, your blessings, your eternity, heaven or hell, are all in your own mouth.

Note this: Romans 10:17, "Faith comes by hearing and hearing the Word of God." So in your own speaking and praying, always SAY it so your own ears can "hear" it. So what have you been saying all the time? Your own mouth can either increase your faith, or it can keep you where you are now. Are you in the same "state of mind" as you were this time last year? What are your habits with your tongue, the way you respond for whatever situation? Do you seem to be the same emotionally day by day, yes, even during spurts of pleasure from sports, sex, parties, etc.? Remember the old saying, "to expect change by doing the same thing over and over......that's a definition of insanity." So change what your mouth says to better words of encouragement, of forgiveness, of love, of healing, of better finances, not blaming others, and much more. If it slips sometimes, as it probably will, use 1 John 1:9 to ask for forgiveness from God, which He readily gives, and then keep on keeping on. Also, stay humble, ask others to forgive you, and you forgive them. Keep praying for your ears to hear you speak with the Authority of the Name of Jesus. The more you do it, then next year you will have changed to God's Way a whole lot more with a better "state of mind."

Lastly, the main purpose of this chapter was for you to get to know more of who you are in Christ. The more you give your time, your money, your prayers, your reading, your improved speaking, and in you doing righteous things, the more God will make sure of this verse onto you, Luke 6:38, "Give and it will be given to you: good measure, shaken together, and running over will be put into your bosom. For with the same measure that you use, it will be measured back to you." The more you receive the more effective you will be where it will be witnessed by others who will gain more interest in God, because of your example of the words coming from your own mouth and the visible results of His works of healing, casting out demons, and much more through you doing "the works of Jesus and greater works."

CHAPTER 3

EFFECTIVE PRAYERS

My prayer life started from day one when I became a Christian in 1981. In 1987 I got a pamphlet, "Your Guide to Successful Prayer," by Larry Lea, which mainly expands "The Lord's Prayer", in Matthew 6:9-13. See, I didn't know how to pray in the beginning. But like I have written in this book, "Fake it till you make it". Do something, then do it again, and soon you will become more effective. Over the years, because of a lot of reading and listening, I added bits and pieces, and eliminated some due to increased wisdom. One major thing is that I saw many prayers right in the Bible, giving me better wording. I knew that what is in the Bible is Truth yesterday, today, and forever. So I made them personal for me with some additional words here and there for clarity. You will understand as you read. This chapter reveals most of my prayers that I would do daily, privately, in my "prayer closet", a place where there is little to no distractions from the world. Some days I would do shorter 'versions', because of just life happening. Pay close attention to all the words as you read and imagine most of them becoming a major part of who you are "in Christ". These verses are not for memorizing as so many do, but especially, it is the Word of God being 'cemented' into your heart. Also, as you adapt any or all of these prayers, put them in the order that you are comfortable. Also, remember Proverbs 6:2, interpreted this way: "SAY what you want, not what you don't want."

For this first prayer, I added for your benefit, the Bible references, some translated out of Bible Concordances, but I don't say the references while I pray, and you will have to determine how to pronounce them:

I say, "Hallowed be all thy Names. Thank you, Father

>for being my Jehovah-tsidkenu, My Lord of Righteousness (Jer 23:6),

>for being my Jehovah-m'kaddesh, My Lord of Sanctification (Lev 20:7&8),

>for being my Jehovah-shalom, My Lord of Peace, nothing broken nor missing (Judg 6:24),

>for being my Jehovah-shammah, My Lord who is always there with never ending love, never ending forgiveness, never ending mercy, and never ending grace. (Ezek 48:35),

>for being my Jehovah-rophe, My Lord of Healing (Ex 15:26),

>for being my Jehovah-jireh, My Lord my Provider, where there's no shortage (Gen 22:14),

>for being my Jehovah-nissi, My Lord, my Banner of victory against the Babylonian System of this "world". (Ex 17:15),

for being my Jehovah-rohi, My Lord, My Sheppard, My Father, who's first in my life, giving me stability. (Ps 23:1),

for being my Jehovah-sabaoth, My Lord of Hosts, with armies for protection and assistance for me. (1 Sam 17:45),

for being my Jehovah-bara, My Lord my Creator. (Is 40:28), for being my Jehovah-elyon, My Lord Most High. (Gen 14:18),

for being my Jehovah-hamakom, My Lord of the place of your Habitation for me. (Ps 91:9),

and for being my El-Shaddai, My all sufficient God Who's more than enough, Who's omniscient (all knowing), Who's omnipotent (all powerful), Who's omnipresent (present everywhere, past, present, and future), and Who's omni-benevolent (always Good), and Who's just, perfect, righteous, merciful, infinite, sovereign, My God of Love with never ending Grace, and much, much more for me to experience being one with You Father, for eternity."

A second prayer (it is a general, but thorough prayer):

"Father, I commit into Your Hands myself, your servant. I yield myself to You, and I plead the blood of Jesus....in my weakness to be my strength, in my not knowing to be my assurance that I know and do righteously, and to cause me to walk BOLDLY in the footsteps You've already prepared for me, and to pour out upon me the Spirit of Your anointing, with all my prayers, teaching, and writing coming out of Your Spirit in the epicenter of my body, that I will fulfill your

CHARGE, and to guide me, protect me, and prepare my hands and mouth to GO and TELL to the people you lead me to, and to bless and keep me, with the help of my Angels in charge over me, and to cause the Light of Your Favor to shine upon me, also for others to see, and to spread over my life the dwelling of your manifested Glory, Christ in me, and to shelter me in the covering of Your Grace...... all done in the Name of the Anointed One, Jesus......and I believe I receive all of this prayer."

Another prayer: Ephesians 1: 17-23 (remember I made it personal for me):

"I pray to you the God of My Lord Jesus Christ, the Father of Glory, to give unto me the Spirit of wisdom and revelation in the knowledge of Him, the eyes of my understanding being enlightened that I may know, with working understanding, what is the hope of His calling for me, to know what is the wealth of His glorious inheritance found in me to fulfill His divine purposes for me, and to know what is the exceeding greatness of His Power TO ME, who believes, according to the working of His mighty Power which You wrought in Christ, when You raised Him from the dead, and set Him at Your own right Hand in the heavenly places. So I am made to be together with You, Jesus, far above all principality, and power, and might, and dominion, and every name that is named, not only in this world, but also in that which is to come. And You have put all things under His feet and gave Him to be head over all things to the Church, which is His body, the fullness of Him that filleth all in all. Hallelujah, I am part of that 'fullness'."

(Then read Ephesians 2:1, then 2:4-7):

"And me you made alive when I was dead in trespasses and sins. But God, You who are rich in mercy, because of your great love with which You loved me, even when I was dead in sin, made me alive together with Christ (by Grace I was saved), and raised me up together and made me to sit together in the heavenly places IN Christ Jesus, that in the ages to come You, God, might show the exceeding riches of Your Grace in Your kindness toward us in Christ Jesus. Lord, I accept Thy gracious word. I believe that Thou hast thus wrought for me. In humble faith I do now take my seat in the heavenly places in Christ Jesus at thy right hand. Teach me how to fulfill this sacred ministry, how to exercise the authority which thou hast entrusted to me. Train me day by day that I may attain to the full stature of the perfect man in Christ, so that in me Thy PURPOSE OF THE AGES may be fulfilled. Thank you for guiding me in that purpose You have for me with 100% effectiveness in all I do in You. And as I continue to abide closely in You, in heavenly places, my prayers for the advancement of the Kingdom has manifested the exercise of a Spiritual Authority that recognizes no national or physical boundaries, but fearlessly binds the forces of darkness in any part of the world to advance the Kingdom."

(Then read Ephesians 3: 14-21):

"For this cause I bow my knees unto You, my Father of our Lord Jesus Christ, from whom the whole family in heaven and earth is named, that You would grant me, according to the riches of Your glory, to be strengthened with might by Your Spirit in my inner man; that Christ may dwell in my heart by faith that I, being rooted and grounded in Your love may be able to comprehend with all the saints what is the breath, and length, and depth, and height to know intimately and thoroughly, the Love of You, Jesus, which passes knowledge giving me a heavenly knowing deep in my spirit, and I am filled with ALL the fullness of You God. Now You are able to do exceeding abundantly above all that I ask or think according the power that works in me to do the greater works of Jesus."

(Then read this):

"So I am conscious 24/7 of my occupation, holding my place of authority in my seat in heavenly places; abiding steadfastly by faith by being arrayed in my full Armor constituting my protection fully kept and unhampered, and giving my PLACE entire attention to do Your Works on a level of power the world does not understand with NO suggestion of defeat, secure in my Armor, and disregarding the enemy!"

(Here is another one to read, Mark 16: 17 & 18):

"And these signs will follow to me who believes: In Jesus Name I will cast out demons; I speak with new tongues; I will take up serpents; and if I eat or drink anything deadly, it will by no means hurt me; I will lay hands on the sick and they will recover."

(Then read Phil 4: 6,7, and 19, here is where you can list your requests and needs):

"I am anxious for nothing, but in everything by prayer and supplication, with thanksgiving, I let my requests be made known to You God; and the peace of God, which surpasses all understanding, will guard my heart and mind through Christ Jesus. And my God shall supply all my needs according to His riches in glory by Christ Jesus." (list your needs here).

(Now here is one of my most important prayers: Psalms 91 to read):

"I dwell in the secret place of the most High and abide under the shadow of the Almighty, and I say of the Lord: You are my refuge and my fortress, my God in You I trust. Surely you shall deliver me from the snare of the fowler, and from the deadly pestilence. You shall cover me with your feathers and under your wings shall I trust, your truth shall be my shield and buckler. So, I shall not be afraid of the terror by night, nor for the arrow that flieth by day, nor of the pestilence that walks in the darkness, nor for the destruction that wasteth at noonday. A thousand shall fall at my side, and ten thousand at my right hand, but it shall not come near me. Only with my eyes shall I see the reward of the wicked. And because I have made you Lord, which is my refuge, even the most High, my habitation, no evil shall befall me, no accident shall overtake me, neither shall any plague or calamity come near my dwelling. For You shall give your angels charge over me to keep me in all my ways, and they shall bear me up in their hands before I dash my foot against a stone. I shall tread upon and trample underfoot the lion and the serpent. And because I have set my love upon you, Father, you will deliver me and set me on high, and because I know your Name, when I call upon You, You will answer me and be with me in any trouble and will deliver me and honor me and with long life you will satisfy me and show me Your salvation, Your wholeness."

(More prayers from Isaiah 54:17 and 32:17 & 18, which I have used for years for protection against weapons and storms and any enemy):

"No weapon formed or fashioned against me shall prosper, and every tongue which rises up against me in judgment shall be condemned, proved to be wrong. This is the heritage of the servants of the Lord, and my righteousness comes from You, Lord. The work of righteousness will be peace, and the effect of righteousness quietness and assurance forever. So I dwell in a peaceful habitation, in a secure dwelling, and a quiet resting place under the protection of the blood of Jesus where there's no lightning, hurricane, tornado, theft, or any evil acts of the enemy, or any other kind of damage or calamity shall come against me, my place of dwelling, my family, or my possessions. SO BE IT!"

(A short one from Luke 10:19)

"Thank you, Father, for you have given me the Authority to trample on serpents and scorpions, and over ALL the power of the enemy, and NOTHING SHALL BY ANY MEANS HURT ME!"

(This prayer comes from Ephesians 6, that again, I say every morning. Also, I am adding a prayer about the Blood of Jesus that I learned a long time ago):

"I put on the whole Armor of God which is the Lord, Jesus Christ, that's on me 24/7: I put on the Girdle of Truth, my clear understanding of Your Word, and I stand firm in the Truth of Your Word, so I will not be a victim of Satan's lies.

I put on the Breastplate of Righteousness, my active obedience of Your Word. My heart loves that which is righteous, and I refuse that which is sinful. Thank you for the imputed righteousness of Christ, as my sins were crucified with you, Jesus, making me right with God.

By faith, I put on the Shoes of Peace, my active ministry of proclaiming Your Word. Help me to stand firm in Christ's victory today. Help me be a peacemaker and not a troublemaker.

By faith, I take the Shield of Faith to quench all the fiery darts of Satan. Help me not to add fuel to any of Satan's darts. Thank you that I can go into this day without fear, where I have complete refuge under the Blood of Jesus that no power of the enemy can penetrate.

By faith, I put on the Helmet of Salvation. I have Your covering and Your mind, Jesus. I remember today that you're coming again soon, help me live for the future tense, and I command in Jesus Name, for my mind to be void of any unrighteousness.

By faith, I take the two edged Sword of Your Word to be ready in my hands so I can expose any temptations from Satan."

(Now the prayer of Jabez who is first mentioned in 1 Chronicles 2:55):

"Oh, that You would bless me indeed and enlarge my territory, that Your hand would be with me, and that You would keep me from evil, that I may not cause pain! (1 Chronicles 4:10). One thing I have desired of the Lord, that I will seek. That I may dwell in the house of the Lord all the days of my life, to behold the beauty of the Lord, and to inquire in His temple (Psalm 27:4). I am righteous, have a renewed mind, walk in faith, and have joy and peace in believing. (Romans 15:13). The fruit of the Spirit abides in me: love, peace, patience, kindness, goodness, faithfulness, gentleness, and self-control (Gal 5:22-23). I have the spirit of wisdom and revelation in the knowledge of God (Eph 1:17). I am seated in heavenly places (Eph 2:6). It is no longer I who lives but Christ who lives in me (Gal 2:20). I walk in humility (Phil 2:5-11). I look great. I feel great. I weigh what God calls me to weigh. I walk in perfect health. I am youthful and energetic. I sleep well. I will see great acceleration in my life. The blessings and favor of God overtake me. I am at the right place at the right time, meeting the right people; doing the things I'm supposed to do. Every seed I have sown, the Lord is bringing a reward and a harvest to me. This is the time of double portion. Release the promises, the breakthroughs, the unexpected, and the suddenly over my life. I walk in the anointing, seeing the Lord work great signs, wonders, and miracles as well as a mass salvation of souls coming to Jesus."

PROPHETIC DECREES FOR DIVINE ENCOUNTERS

"I am patient and kind. I do not envy, parade myself and am not puffed up. I do not behave rudely, do not seek my own, am not provoked and think no evil. I do not rejoice in iniquity, but rejoice in the truth. I bear all things, believe all things, hope all things, and endure all things. I never fail. (1 Corinthians 13).

I am loved. The Lord loves me, delights in me. I am accepted. I belong. I am significant. I love the Lord with all my heart, soul, mind, and strength. I have passion for Jesus and am awakened in revelation about being His bride. The first commandment is my first priority. The Lord is my shepherd, my leader, my provider who is responsible for me. I shall not lack anything that is needed in doing God's will. God's goodness and mercy continues all my days. He leads me in the right path to fulfill His will. The Lord will be a wall of fire all around me, and He will be the glory in my midst. (Zechariah 2:5). The Lord protects (insert the name of your spouse), myself and our children. We walk in fullness of health and healing. No weapon formed against us shall prosper and every tongue that rises against us in judgment, you shall condemn. This is the heritage of the servants of the Lord and their righteousness is from Me, says the Lord." (Isaiah 54:17).

Another prayer from Genesis 12:3:

"I will bless those who bless you {Israel}, and I will curse those who curse you; and all the families of the earth shall be blessed," and from Psalm 122:6: "I pray for the peace of Jerusalem; may they prosper who love you." (Remember that we Christians are heirs of Abraham through accepting Jesus, therefore, adopted Jews.)

"Father, I pray for the peace of Jerusalem. I ask You to keep Israel in your loving care. Thank You for a spiritual and physical hedge of protection around your people and the United States Embassy and its occupants. I pray for the eternal preservation of their land, including the confounding and confusion and destruction of the many plots of the enemy against Israel, and that all of the evil works against Israel be defeated with the help of your angel armies, as You did in her past. Watch over this nation as a Good Shepard watches over His flock, and may Your chosen people find their ultimate safety and security in You. And may your Spirit awaken in them a hunger to embrace their Messiah, Jesus, for their salvation."

Another prayer that I have said for years:

"I decree my eyes are blessed, I can see. My ears are blessed, I can hear. I perceive and understand what Your Spirit is saying to me. I have Your mind Jesus. I have been made Your righteousness. I am Your servant, soldier, co-worker, and disciple, becoming like You. I have an anointing from the Holy Spirit, and I know everything I need to know, AS I need to know it. Revelation flows in me and through me. Greater is He that is in me than he who is in the world, and I can do all things through Christ which strengthens me, since Christ is in me!" (1 John 4:4 & Phil 4:13).

In conclusion of this chapter on prayers, realize that it is up to you that "choose" to begin a daily life of prayer, how, and in what order, you may want to use any or all these prayers.

Also, you don't have to repeat all these all the time. You can schedule different days for different ones. But the more you SAY them from your heart, consistently, day by day, you are putting, for the most part, God's Words into your heart so that it becomes part of WHO you are as a new creature IN CHRIST. Again, from your heart say them, not just repetitions of words. "Feel" them in your heart as you SAY them, as they will, in time, reflect what you say.

CHAPTER 4

ARTICLES WRITTEN ABOUT THE WORLD VERSUS JESUS

This chapter contains several articles that I have written in the past (with a little repetition, because they were written at different time frames, sometimes years apart) as examples of how I addressed, basically, God's Word versus whatever "world" subject was being discussed. I have thousands in my archives as I have been writing since 2008. But this is my first book. The reason to include these few articles is because of the enemy, the "world," is still "off track", but God's Truth is still valid, even though we are in the "21st Century", where many have been deceived that society should be different now. Many of my articles came as a result from email, Facebook, and stuff on TV about material that was quite misleading to the "unknowing" of God and His Word. Many times the answer to my article would come back with anger and hate trying to justify themselves. I mainly answered back in truth and love, because others were also reading. I had discussions with atheists, agnostics, scientologists, gays, Muslims, liberalists, democrats, socialists, and others. Many were very "intelligent" from the "world's" point of view, and they would call me the opposite, with a little vulgarity……..but the truth prevailed. And some articles were written just for teaching God's Word.

Article One: It's so simple about God's love, but normal man can't comprehend……totally.

God, the great, I AM, of eternity past, present, and future, invented time for man. Out of Who He is, LOVE, God gave man "free will" to choose love, which Adam and Eve lived with "Heaven on earth" a while in the Garden of Eden.

But Satan interfered with them and brought sin and death into this world. So man has been born with a sin nature since then and up to now. We still have, though, "free will", that's so critical to God. Why? ….to be answered in the last two paragraphs. That sin nature led man into ALL wars, strife, disease, racism, sinful anger, theft, homosexuality, many other sexual problems, pornography, killing babies, being power hungry, and "riches" hunger, murder, destruction of property, and much, much more. Which, or, how many are yours? This goes for me, too.

But…but…but…GOD!!!!!! God, who is still the one and only living God, I AM, out of His incomprehensible LOVE, brought His only Son, Jesus (sinless), to die on the cross with ALL that sin, death, disease, and poverty on His back to be rid of it permanently, by taking it all to hell and be given back to Satan and taking the keys for all that, be resurrected, and ascended to heaven…..all to bring man back to what He created for man, the free will choice of LOVE.

So why does man still suffer with ALL the results of that sin nature? It's simple…..He does not USE his "free will" to BELIEVE

WHAT GOD DID WITH JESUS, confess with his mouth and ask for Jesus to come into his life, and ask for forgiveness of ALL his sins (past, present, and future) (Rom 10:9 and 1 John 1:9), so he will receive salvation (healing, lack of poverty, and deliverance). Realize that your spirit will receive the Holy Spirit, but the mind and body have to get to KNOW Jesus in order to receive these total blessings.

But most of mankind really doesn't much believe the end result, even though "saved", so they still suffer and sometimes blame God, because they have NOT pursued very much (once a week, if even that, isn't enough) to pursue to KNOW Jesus (Rom 12:2), and to find out about…..

Why God gave man free will…….to LOVE, His Way (put love for God first place with your time and money) and for the rest of his life here on earth, while receiving the blessings of "knowing God", spiritually, physically, and financially, …..to PREPARE doing "the works of Jesus and greater works" (John 14:12) and for what God has planned for His Church for eternity (read and understand Ephesians 2: 4-10).

Article two: Will You Pass the Critical Test?

God created man…….FOR WHAT PURPOSE? Don't miss the "test" in Step 6.

In eternity past, present, and eternity future, the Great God "I Am" exists. God created "time" for man. Compared to eternity past and eternity future, it is but a "speck of time!" A thousand years is as one day with God (2 Peter 3:8), so man has been here for not even a half month.

Out of "love" God created man as the only creature with FREE WILL. Did you ever consider WHY, while we're here in the "present", and for what purpose for the eternal future?

Well, the first step, He wanted man to use His "free will" to "love" Him back.

2nd step: But God knew that sin would enter into the "world" through Satan tempting Adam and Eve by breaking the only existing Law: "Don't eat of the tree of the knowledge of good and evil" (Genesis 2:17). God knew He would send His sinless Son, Jesus, to erase sin by taking it back to the one who started it, Satan.

3rd step: It was set up that man could use his free will to "live" rather than "die" into eternity future by accepting the one and only Plan of God, Jesus, by "confessing with their mouth the Lord Jesus" (Rom 10:9).

So, 4th step, despite man's past, present, and future sins, for those that accepted Jesus, which ones of those will pass the test by taking advantage of the rest of their lives on earth with "their" speck of time to love God back by getting to "know" Him through Jesus while doing all the other requirements of "making a living", despite their sins?

And 5th step, which ones of "those" will pass the test, despite their hindrances, to enter the Glory of God using John 14:12, where Jesus said, "....the works that I do he will do, and greater works will he do", by spreading His Love to others, and/or by spreading the Gospel, and/or healing the sick, and/or getting the lame to walk and the blind to see, the deaf to hear the dumb to speak, and/or raising the dead, and/or casting out devils, and/or some combinations of all this and much more?

And finally, the 6th step, which men and women using their "free will", despite all the challenges of this temporary "world's, speck of time", will consistently stick to step 5, to enter into the realm of the Church that God is going to present in the "ages to come" (Ephesians 2:7), which is eternity future, including the Millennium? The rest of the true church will be included, but those that took what Jesus gave them into that higher realm of step 5 will reap as those "two" in the "Parable of the Talents" (read carefully Matthew 25:14-30).

NOW, THINK, dwell on this…..My omnipresent God created man for much, much more than for this "speck of time" ……He will present His Church for eternity…………………………..FOR WHAT PURPOSE?

Article three: Will your resume qualify for the work God has planned for eternity?

Are you preparing yourself for "what" you will be doing for eternity? Accepting Jesus, with belief, and getting to know Him gets you "into" heaven…..but then what? (I am adding to this article now a thought. See most talk about accepting Jesus to go to heaven is usually where the subject ends. But there is more).

Your vital time on this earth is infinitesimal compared to your eternal life…..or will be your eternal death for those rejecters of

Jesus? How long is eternity again? How much of that is your life here before Jesus comes?

Are you 100% devoted to your family, to sports, the job, etc., and 0% to God? Or do you think your 1% of your time for church (most of which I have observed don't even take their Bible) once a week, or less, is enough to qualify for the work of God's purpose for you for eternity?

How much of your money and weekly time do you make for studying His Word, praying, helping people, spreading the Gospel, healing, and much, much more?

I am mainly referring to the "focusing" of your mind as all your days progress on this earth till Jesus comes. See God knows your schedule. He knows how to multiply your time and money spent with/for Him more than it would have with nothing given to Him. Even Apostle Paul pretty much worked where ever he went doing God's Work.

And both know that during all the time/money focused for God, you will go from tribulations, to perseverance, to character and to hope (Romans 5: 3 & 4). The hope is KNOWING Him (don't forget the critical Matthew 7: 21-23…..does He "know" you?) and His coming as a fact, but it's the character you develop during the process that is the "qualifier" for that "resume".

All your sins are not even in that resume, either, as long as you accepted Jesus.

So, do you…..or will you qualify in the resume to be part, at whatever level of responsibility, of His Church, that, "in the ages to come (eternity) He might SHOW the exceeding riches of His Grace….?" (Ephesians 2:7, parenthesis and caps mine).

Look all through the Bible what God has done to engineer the forming of His Church, not a religion, through Jesus Christ! Not just to get to heaven, which is most important, but God has work for His Church (the people, not the building) for eternity. Now….. let your imaginations wonder…..doing what?

Article four: Once saved, always saved?

Per the salvation verse, Romans 10:9, you accept Jesus as your savior for all sins: past, present, and future.

Many Christians claim the "Once saved, always saved" phrase, no matter what they do with their life after accepting Jesus. So here is some discussion:

How many Christians have sinned since they were saved? Try….. ALL! Remember even lying is a sin…pride is a sin…un-forgiveness is a sin. Mark 11:26, paraphrased, "If you don't forgive (even for your own relatives), how can God forgive you?" Pride is the worst sin. It got Lucifer kicked out of heaven to become Satan.

If you have thoughts of adultery, you have committed it (Matthew 5:28). Proverbs 6:2: "Thou are snared by the words of your mouth (this gets most into trouble all the time)." I can bring up many more examples of sin easily done, even by Christians.

Now, we do have 1 John 1:9, "If we confess our sins (even after you're saved, and especially as quick as you can after 'fouling up'), He is faithful and just to forgive us our sins and cleanse us from all unrighteousness." How often are you doing this…..even daily?

If not, John 10:10 puts you in jeopardy, "The thief (the devil) does not come except to steal (anyone steal from you lately?), kill (a reason some die un-expectantly), and to destroy (does your life get messed up a lot?)"…..So the Devil (Satan), or his demons, will take

advantage quickly, sometimes, for any unconfessed sins, even without your awareness, and not always immediately after (ever wonder why bad things seem to happen to good people?....It might be for something you did last year).

Even righteous Christians will struggle, because the Devil is after them, too, but for those well into the Word (read Rom 12:2), they know they have power in the Name of Jesus to cast him away, even illnesses, and retain peace.

Another point: per Revelation 3: 15 & 16, God said He will "spit out" the lukewarmers, the compromisers: those (even Christians) who fall for the world's ways of abortion, homosexuality, socialism, and much more, because they have no solid foundation of God and His Word, and they want to say they are Christian, but support sin, hence, lukewarmers.

Finally, just sticking to the "Once saved, always saved" without living by Matthew 6:33, "Seek Ye first, etc.", makes you prey for missing out on those "things" you need, and per Philippians 4:6&7, the "peace that surpasses all understanding".

So, if you have been sticking only to "Once saved, always saved"...... ever wonder why you have so many struggles physically, and/or spiritually, and/or financially, and/or emotionally?

Will you still go to heaven? God knows your heart, and still loves you, but that's why He sent Jesus, for you to not only accept Him, but to get to KNOW Him through praying, forgiveness, and seeking His Word......opening up the door for His purpose for you.

So, it is in your hands..... "Once saved, always saved?????????"

Article five: Why will the God of Love send people to hell?

Extra for this article: First of all, this will not actually happen till the "Great White Throne Judgment", Revelation 20:11-15, where ALL that had rejected Jesus up to just before He came to "take us up", gets judged by God, and their spirit eternally goes into spiritual death with torment.

DON'T MISS THE LAST PARAGRAPH....THE ANSWER.

There is a rampant deception increasing exponentially in the "world" about this subject having good success in convincing people that God isn't real. But that is due to the Master of Deception, yes, Satan himself.

This is another case of "people don't know what they don't know", so they go with their "intellect" based on what others have said, and it makes sense to the "unknowing".

Remember God gave man free will. And due to Adam's sin under the influence of that same Satan, sin was brought into the world. So all mankind is born with that sin nature.

Now God and sin cannot coexist together. There are so many references in the Word. Sin got Satan kicked out of heaven, it caused the flood in Noah's time, the destruction of Sodom and Gomorrah, and much more, and it is why God turned His back on Jesus "after" putting the sin of all mankind past, present, and future onto Jesus's back, thereby shedding His blood for All.

The wages of sin is death (Romans 6:23). So since Jesus was sinless, He took all that sin into hell to give it back to Satan, then was resurrected, being sinless, therefore, there illegally. And through that blood spilled covenant, God set it up, because of His love, for any that chose to believe that Jesus did that for them, and asked for forgiveness for all their sin, so that afterwards God would only see Jesus in them, they had the legal right to be with Him for eternal life……no more spiritual death.

So, even though God loves you, He gave you free will to choose His Way, Jesus, for eternal Life. And 2 things for these people that just can't seem to fathom this:

1. There's no way for your body, still with the sin nature, could be with God, BECAUSE YOU WOULD BE DESTROYED AUTOMATICALLY, because God and sin cannot COEXSIST.
2. AND GOD WOULD NOT BE GOD ANYMORE, THEREFORE NEVER WAS......THEREFORE, MAN AND THE UNIVERSE WOULD NOT EXIST AT ALL!

Article six: Why do you get sick? You were healed before you were born!

Remember when Jesus died on the cross every disease, sickness, infirmity, poverty, sin and death, etc., was put on Him. He took them to hell and gave it back to Satan. This was God's only Plan, so all mankind would have the WAY for Salvation (wholeness) through Jesus and receive eternal life.

So all of mankind was born healed, but you have to accept Jesus to RECEIVE that healing, but don't be concerned about your dirty past. Join the Club of the rest of us Christians. God wants you to run TO Him, not away from Him. But, even then, most don't know HOW to get healed. It's not, so much, by "asking" God for something He has already given. It's by commanding it and "receiving it" by the Authority of the Name of Jesus.

Show me anywhere in the Bible where Jesus says you have to wait until it is His Will.

Jesus, nor any of His disciples, had anyone "wait"......that believed. So it is by faith.....believing. Read Mark 16:17 & 18......if you believe. And God gives every true believer of Jesus the "measure of faith" (Romans 12:3).

"Choosing" to believe activates what your born again spirit ALREADY KNOWS....by SAYING it. "Faith comes by hearing, and hearing BY THE Word of God" (Romans 10:17). Your own ears have to hear what your mouth is saying. Keep SAYING His Word with belief. Do it repeatedly until that belief becomes a reality (sort of... fake it till you make it....the way I started.....and it's better than not at all). Do this process to receive healing, prosperity, more understanding of His Word, the answer to prayers, etc.

Our reborn spirit is perfect, but it takes humans 'X' amount of time to get their minds and body to catch up to "receive it." The world was created by the SPOKEN Word. Jesus used spoken words in everything He did. And He said in John 14:12 that we would "do His works, and even greater works will we do."

There is a multitude of verses, as I wrote earlier, in the Bible to make it personal for you in your prayers to "speak" it into reality, by declaring it with your mouth (and God is no respecter of persons): Mark 16:17 & 18, Ephesians 1:17-23, then 2:4-7, Ephesians 3:14-21, Luke 6: 38, Col 1:12 & 13, 2 Tim 4:18, Luke 10:19, James 4:7, 2 Tim 1:7, Psalm 91, Psalm 23, 1 Thess 5:23, James 1:5, Rom 8:37, 2 Cor 6:2b, and much more. Try praying some or all these verses daily, personal to you.

Get ready for the "ages to come" (Eph 2:7), by preparing yourself with your time still here on earth.....or live in doubt and sickness and worry of wondering about your "future" status....but....but....but....what if you're NOT born again?

Article seven: Your conscience generates your own fear.

A revelation: If you avoid the truth of God and say it is fear based (this is a common response from the unrighteous),.....then you're living in self produced fear. But due to pride, you talk against the one speaking His truth by using slander. And with this world's "intelligence" that slander can be very intricately wicked.

Example from a loved one who wrote about me: "The dangerous place you're in is due to your isolation, lack of input and opinion from a variety of sources, and extreme thinking. I truly feel you're a religious terrorist ...a person who frightens others...intended to create fear...." But in his report there was much more "slander", but with the conclusion of "unconditional" love for me. But his "conditional" love is that I have NO communication with him until he is sure that my "unconditional" doesn't include God???? But my "unconditional" love for him is that I want him with me for eternity. Well, every day I remind myself that he is in God's hands.

From a man of God: "Folks, as we rush faster and faster into the final days of this Age of Grace, I'm reminded of what Habakkuk lamented, 'The wicked surround the righteous; Therefore, justice comes out perverted.' (Habakkuk 1:4, NASB) This will be the order of the day until Jesus Christ returns to snatch away those who have accepted His free gift of pardon."

See with the conscience that God gives all, you KNOW He is RIGHT, but your sin nature wants to rule, and though God loves you, He cannot coexist with your unconfessed sin.

I pray for ALL my loved ones to accept the absolute and only Truth of God's plan of Salvation: Jesus.

(A note separate from this article: I included it, because I know that many of the righteous people of God have had and still do have similar experiences from loved ones…..you are not alone).

Article eight: Spiritual Authority.

This part is extracted from a Sunday School series of articles titled, Growth Track, with my church in Pensacola, Florida. Read and SEE WHY the Authority of the Name of Jesus is so critical to the point that it separates basically the "once a week "Christians" from the Christians that do the "works of Jesus and greater works".

When we begin to pray we begin to go against the plans of the Devil and he gets angry. If he has any access to your life or the lives of those around you he will begin to attack. Furthermore, as you begin to exercise more of your AUTHORITY in the kingdom you come up against demons you haven't met yet.

All authority has been given to Jesus. When we accept Him as Lord and savior we receive His authority and must begin to walk in His authority. As a new Christian this may be hard if you don't KNOW His Word or His directives towards us. The devil will use our lack of knowledge to keep us Christians in pain, misery and suffering. The devil wants to keep Christians from understanding the power that they have been given by God.

As God and creator, all authority belongs to Jesus. "For thus says the Lord, Who created the heavens, Who is God, Who formed the earth and made it, Who has established it, Who did not create it in vain, Who formed it to be inhabited: I am the Lord, and there is no other." (Isaiah 45:18). "And Jesus came and spoke to them saying, 'All authority has been given to Me in heaven and on earth.' (Matthew 28:18)." "Therefore God also has highly exalted Him and given Him the name which is above every name, that at the name of Jesus every Knee should bow, of those in heaven, and those on earth, and of those under the earth, and that every tongue should confess that Jesus Christ is Lord, to the glory of God the Father. (Phil 2: 9-11)"

His authority has been extended to us and He expects us to use it. Here are some verses to bring it alive for our knowledge:

> "God said, 'Let us make man in Our image, according to Our likeness; let them have dominion

over the fish of the sea, over the birds of the air, and over the cattle, over all the earth and over every creeping thing that creeps on the earth." (Genesis 1:26). Remember that Satan stole it from Adam, but through Jesus, we take it back: "...and God raised us up together, and made us sit together in the heavenly places in Christ Jesus." (Ephesians 2:6).

"No weapon formed against you shall prosper." (Isaiah 54:17).

"....and on this rock (of Jesus) I will build My church, and the gates of Hades shall not prevail against it." (Matthew 16:18, parenthesis mine from the concordance of the word 'rock', and Peter, the 'rock' is translated, a 'piece' of the rock).

"And I will give you the keys of the kingdom, and whatever you bind on earth will be bound in heaven, and whatever you loose on earth will be loosed in heaven." (Matthew 16:19).

"Behold, I give you the authority to trample on serpents and scorpions, and over all the power of the enemy, and nothing shall by any means hurt you" (Luke 10:19).

"Therefore submit to God, resist the devil and he will flee from you" (James 4:7).

"Most assuredly, I say to you, he who believes in Me, the works that I do he will do also; and greater works than these he will do, because I go to my Father." (John 14:12).

The authority of God is required to build His kingdom and to push back the works of the enemy. So every day with your mouth, say that I: "Put on the whole armor of God, that ('I') may be able to stand against the wiles of the devil. For ('I') do not wrestle against flesh and blood, but against principalities, against powers, against the rulers of the darkness of this age, against spiritual hosts of wickedness in the heavenly places." (Ephesians 6: 11-12).

"For though we walk in the flesh, we do not war according to the flesh, for the weapons of our warfare are not of the flesh, but divinely powerful for the pulling down of strongholds." (2 Corinthians 10:3-5). So you, in Christ, have the authority to break all curses of sickness and death. So, "Go into all the world and preach the gospel to every creature. He who believes and is baptized will be saved; but he who does not believe will be condemned. And these signs will follow those who believe: In My name they will cast out demons; they will speak with new tongues; they will take up serpents; and if they drink anything deadly, it will by no means hurt them; they will lay hands on the sick, and they will recover." (Mark 16: 15-18).

"The thief comes only to steal and kill and destroy." (John 10:10). The reasons for the problems that man encounters is the "nature" of this world under Satan who wants them to stay "ignorant" through several ways:

1. People maintain the spirit of "me", rather than submitting to God, like holding onto the past, un-forgiveness, letting pride rule, focusing on their problems like poverty, sickness, etc.
2. Practicing "religion", and not focusing on getting to KNOW Jesus, daily, not just once a week.
3. Letting demons have their way....mainly, because they don't KNOW Jesus, they don't recognize when it is demons.

4. Letting their own mouth have its way, like saying "I'm sick", instead of saying, "I'm healed", and much, much more damaging things of "confessing" problems into their lives.
5. Lack of consistent, daily organized praying. "The one concern of the devil is to keep Christians from praying. He fears nothing from prayerless studies, prayerless, work, and prayerless religion. He laughs at our toil, mocks at our wisdom, but he trembles when we Pray." Samuel Chadwick.

CHAPTER 5

MORE OF THE BIBLE REVEALED

Again, I am writing to let you know more of what I have learned in the process of getting to KNOW Jesus. All this writing is NOT to impress you with my knowledge, but to encourage you to pursue the process to get to KNOW Jesus with what He reveals to you so that YOU would "do the works of Jesus and greater works". Also, you will gain more wisdom of how to deal with the situations you, or your family, or your relatives, co-workers, and neighbors may encounter.

I will start with some Parables that Jesus taught that contain a wealth of information to bring more wisdom of KNOWING JESUS.

PARABLE OF THE SOWER

The verses Matthew 13: 3-9, you can read, but verses 18-23 explain the meaning: "Therefore hear the parable of the sower: When anyone hears the word of the kingdom and does not understand it, the wicked one comes and snatches away what was sown in his heart. This is he who received seed by the wayside. But he who received the seed on stony places, this is he who hears the word and immediately receives it with joy; yet he has no root in himself, but endures only for a while, for when tribulation or persecution arises because of the word, immediately he stumbles. Now he who received seed among the thorns is he who hears the word; and the cares of this world and the deceitfulness of riches choke the word, and he becomes unfruitful. But he who received seed on good ground is he who hears the word and understands it, who indeed bears fruit and produces ; some a hundred fold, some sixty, and some thirty."

Many Christians have experienced some of each of the different ways we received the seed of God's Word based on our level of time devotion, therefore, different levels of understanding during our process of renewing our minds. But few have stayed consistent with the deep desire to want to KNOW to have reached the "good ground" of Christ awareness predominate in our mind instead of self-awareness. Good ground is to be like a "sponge" soaking into their mind with the desire to want to KNOW the Word, but more important, what God wants them to do and say daily, and just how to USE it in their lives.

THE PARABLE OF THE TALENTS

This is my favorite of parables. Look for an answer of "why bad things happen to 'good' people," in Matthew 25: 14-30: "For the kingdom of heaven is like a man traveling to a far country, who called his own servants and delivered his goods to them. And to one he gave five talents, to another two, and to another one, to each according to his own ability (their past achievements), and immediately he went on a journey.

Then he who had received the 5 talents went and traded with them, and made another five talents. And likewise he who had received two gained two more also. But he who received one went and dug in the ground, and hid his lord's money. After a long time the lord of those servants came and settled accounts with them.

So he who had received five talents came and brought five other talents, saying, 'Lord you delivered to me five talents; look, I have gained five more talents besides them.' His lord said to him, 'Well done good and faithful servant; you were faithful over a few things, I will make you ruler over many things. Enter into the joy of your lord.' He also who had received two talents came and said, 'Lord, you delivered to me two talents; look, I have gained two more talents besides them.' His lord said to him, 'Well done, good and faithful servant; you have been faithful over a few things, I will make you ruler over many things. Enter into the joy of the lord.'

Then he who had received the one talent came and said, 'Lord I knew you to be a hard man reaping where you have not sown, and gathering where you have not scattered seed. And I was afraid and went and hid your talent in the ground. Look, there you have what is yours.' But his lord answered and said to him, 'You wicked and lazy servant, you knew that I reap where I have not sown, and gather where I have not scattered seed. Therefore, you ought to have deposited my money with the bankers, and at my coming I would have received back my own with interest.

Therefore take the talent from him, and give it to him who has ten talents. For to everyone that has, more will be given, and he will have abundance; but from him who does not have, even what he has will be taken away. And cast the unprofitable servant into the outer darkness. There will be weeping and gnashing of teeth.' "(this is eternal hell).

Now this whole parable is a 'picture' of the age of the church that started on the Day of Pentecost (Acts 2), and we are still in this age till Jesus (the lord comes back from his long journey) comes. So it is our life! What do we do with it as a whole? Go along with the world's way, without God, and where, as in the USA, the liberals want to give government's money to the 'lazy' (welfare)? In 2 Thess 3:10, God said, "....if anyone will not work, neither shall he eat." It is the church's responsibility to take care of the poor, as we are doing in Kenya, not the Government. Or, at least, we should, accept Jesus, who has 'talents' (His Word), to USE what He gives to make progress of how to use it to receive much more than what we put our time and money into and eventually to not only be like Jesus (He made us in His 'likeness), but to "do His works and greater works". Don't you want Jesus to say after He comes to "take us up", "well done, thy good and faithful servant"? Then in the millennium, He will "make us rulers over many things (plans for us for eternity)!"

Also, maybe you can understand, "why bad things seem to happen to good people." See, they 'look' good as the world sees them: good job, good family that maybe goes to church once a week putting a dollar in the offering plate, or for sure at Easter and Christmas, supports the kids in sports, has nice cars and clothes 'in style' for the whole family, buying their kids every new i-phone that comes out, probably has large credit card debt (there was a time in my past where people bragged about having a lot of credit cards), etc. But they have NOT invested much time in the 'talents' that God has given. "…even what he has shall be taken away."

Now we know there are people very much into God's Word where things happen, because they are what the enemy hates the worst. Remember, that enemies' goal is to "steal, kill, and destroy" (John 10:10). But they should still know how to "rebuke the devourer" (Mal 3:11), before the event of: "even what he has shall be taken away." And he should be using the Authority of the Name of Jesus everyday knowing that the enemy wants victory over him.

There are several other parables and many more stories with great 'lessons' that bring us 'seekers' to KNOW Jesus in all the gospels of Matthew, Mark, Luke, and John, but also, the rest of the Bible.

THE RAPTURE VERSUS THE ANTICHRIST

First, I know that due to their 'religion', many don't believe in the 'Rapture'. Some just neglect the following due to the 'pride of their religion' that has avoided this for years. I have witnessed another religion that avoids the Book of Revelation. Why? The WHOLE Bible was written by God! Then some use the reasoning that the word 'rapture' is not in the Bible. But it is the translation of "being taken up, or caught up". Read 1 Corinthians 15:51-53. The trumpet mentioned is, per the Concordance, not the same as in the book of Revelation, which is another study. But, also, read 1 Thessalonians 4: 16 & 17. "For the Lord Himself will descend from heaven with a shout, with the voice of an archangel, and with the trumpet of God. And the dead in Christ will rise first. Then we who are alive and remain shall be caught up together with them in the clouds to meet the Lord IN THE AIR. And thus we shall always be with the Lord." (Caps mine). The Lord will 'catch us up in the clouds, in the air'. It is at the end of the Tribulation, during Armageddon, when the Lord will come 'down to the ground' with His armies (Rev 19).

But now let's study 2 Thessalonians 2: 1-4. "Now, brethren, concerning the coming of our Lord Jesus Christ and our gathering together to Him, we ask you, not to be soon shaken in mind or troubled, either by spirit or by word or by letter, as if from us, as though the day (His return) of Christ had come. Let no one deceive you by any means; for that Day will not come unless the falling away comes first, and the man of sin (the Antichrist) is revealed, the son of perdition, who opposes and exalts himself above all that is called God or that is worshipped, so that he sits as God in the temple of God, showing himself that he is God." (Remember Isaiah 14:12-15 of when Lucifer was kicked out of heaven because of this kind of pride, and became Satan, and now here is the Antichrist, the son of Satan.)

And about the 'falling away', note 1 Timothy 4:1-5, "Now the Spirit expressly says that in the latter times (that Matthew 24 covers showing that those 'times' are now) some will depart from the faith, giving heed to deceiving spirits and doctrines of demons, speaking lies in hypocrisy, having their own conscience seared with a hot iron, forbidding to marry….." NOW, as you can see, the 'falling away' is happening RIGHT NOW around the world, and this will create persecution for those 'in Christ', but we have our 'weapons of warfare' as preparation.

Even as I write this, this is all evidenced by the riots and looting and destruction of other's property in the USA, and also, as witnessed by the corona virus, this fear caused people to pull away from God. Also, as witnessed during this time of mid 2020 in the USA, the media and the 'left' were "giving heed to deceiving spirits and doctrines of demons, speaking lies in hypocrisy" against President Trump. They even created more fear using covid numbers to spread fear. How? It was proven (that media did not cover) that only 1% died of the disease, and that a multitude of other deaths throughout the world were blamed on covid. Why they even said it is okay to riot without social distancing, but you can't have 'church' because of social distance problems……hypocrisy at its best!

A critical point to add here. Call it "conspiracy theory" if you want. I have known for many years that there has been a major 'underground' movement for probably over a hundred years that certain wealthy people have been trying different ways to create a 'One World Government' under a communistic type rule. A "shadow government" was developed to thwart the Republic of the USA. I have heard this several times over the last 3 months of corona, that it was created to produce fear, which leads to control by the governments of the world. I have just discovered that the corona virus was planned in 2010 by those 'one-worlders'. This documented 'plan' from a Rockefeller Foundation article on their website in pdf, had a planned theft to send it to Wuhan that had the only class 4 laboratory in China. It was so detailed that almost everything happening now to school closures, holding back a cure so it would get worse, social distancing, economy failure, businesses closures, media deceptions, church closures (one of their main objectives), and more…..it is happening now! But their other objective was to create a mandatory "vaccine" that would include a chip that 'they' would use to control everyone's life, including buying and selling. I have no idea if the vaccines now in mid-January of 2021 contain this 'chip'. This WILL happen per the book of Revelation called the "Mark of the Beast", but during the Tribulation. But see, for now until we Christians are "taken up", we, in Christ, need to take dominion over any of it coming near us.

Now, back to the 'Rapture' with 2 Thessalonians 7 & 8 (parenthesis mine), "For the mystery of lawlessness is already at work; only He who now restrains (the Holy Spirit, per the concordances) will do so until He is taken out of the way (since the Holy Spirit resides in every true believer that accepted Christ, then the believer has to be taken out of the way, too, hence, the Rapture). And then the lawless one will be revealed….." In Daniel 9:27 (parenthesis mine), "Then he (the lawless one, the Antichrist) shall confirm a covenant (a peace treaty) with the many (Israel) for one (sabbatical) week," This, as you study Daniel 9: 20-27, is that last 7 years, which is called the Tribulation, to be discussed shortly.

So, in summary, the true believers will be "caught up" before the Tribulation. We don't know the exact date, but as I wrote earlier, Matthew 24 discusses these "end days", and the end of the Age, this Church Age, we are in now. These "signs of the end of times" is all around us with increasing frequency, including the "falling away". Also, in this chapter 24, verse 15, reads: "....when you see the "abomination of desolation" ..standing in the Holy place .." (3½ years after the Rapture, the middle of that 7 years, the Antichrist will be trying to be God standing in the temple, which is already being prepared for reconstruction as I write this. This includes all the candles and holders, robes for priests, incense, and much more). The believers will be in heaven going through the "Judgment Seat of Christ" (where we will be judged of what we did and did not do for Christ after our salvation, but not for our sins). We will also be experiencing the joy of the "marriage supper of the Lamb" (Rev 19:9, confirmed in the concordances). A thorough study of Revelation reveals that the "7 years" will be the worst the entire world has ever experienced. I have studied 42 CD's many times on the Book of Revelation by Dr. David Jeremiah, and 19 CD's on the book of Daniel by Hal Lindsey, and both take you into much of the rest of the Bible. Then, per Revelation, we will be in white linen as armies (see the concordances) coming down with Jesus at the end of the 7 years. We will help Jesus rule the world for a thousand years. There will be many that survive the Tribulation. After that, will be the Great White Throne Judgment of God for all those that rejected Jesus. And there is only ONE destination for all of them! The rest of us will spend eternity with God, the Son, and the Holy Spirit doing the NEW works He has already planned!

THE 70 WEEKS IN THE BOOK OF DANIEL

This is a quick snapshot of what is revealed in the book of Daniel about the 70 weeks. He (Daniel) was captured and sent to Babylon when he was a teenager, along with most of all of the people of Israel. There are many great stories of what he went through while becoming a leader in Babylon and a scholar of all the biblical scrolls. When he was much older, maybe in his 80's, he noticed that Israel would soon be in captivity for 70 years where the scrolls had said was the period of time Israel was to be kept in Babylon. So he went and prayed, and asked God to forgive Israel for all her sins (as we should for our country per 2 Chronicles 7:14). Then he prayed to know what is next after that 70 years. The angel, Gabriel, was sent with the answers. This is a short version of one of the greatest 'long period of time' stories in all the Bible, as it prophesizes what was to come in the future of Israel, including up to now, and what is to still come, all of which affects the rest of the world. This is over 400 years BEFORE Jesus.

In the writings of Moses (Leviticus 25), God told Israel to work for 6 years, then rest for one year, so the rest of the world could see how God takes care of His people so that would lead them also to Him. Israel NEVER did that law for 490 years (7 times 70). So God decreed that Israel would be conquered by Babylon and sent there for "70 years", allowing for the land of Israel to be restored. Then back with Daniel and Gabriel, it was decreed that Israel would go back to its land, and as soon as an agreement was made to rebuild Jerusalem, from that day the 'time clock' would be started. Jerusalem would be rebuilt, would be conquered again and again by the Persians, the Greeks, and the Romans. It was the Greeks under Alexander the Great, where he commanded that in all the countries he had conquered all had to learn the Greek language. This is why the New Testament is in Greek, and all, including the Romans and Jews, would be able to communicate.

In Daniel 9, it is written about the 70 weeks, where each week is 7 years called Sabbatical Weeks. The rest of chapter 9 read that there would be 7 weeks (for the rebuilding of Jerusalem), then 62 weeks, which totals 69 weeks. Then the Messiah would be cut off (Crucified), which was the year 33. Then the people of the prince (Satan), which was the Romans, would destroy the city (Jerusalem). That happened in the year 70. This is much more than the 7 years. So only 69 of the 70 years has happened. Then in verse 27, as I wrote earlier, after the signing of the treaty with the Antichrist, the last week of 7 years begins, which is the Tribulation as written in Revelation.

Now I paraphrased and summarized, but have had, as I wrote earlier, much deeper study of all this. I just wanted you to get the point that there is still much more to come. See ALL the prophesies of God has happened on time that was supposed to. So the rest is YET TO COME! God could not be God if this did not happen, which is what Satan is trying to stop.

BEING FORBIDDEN TO EAT CERTAIN FOODS

Since food is on people's mind most of the time, here is some things to consider. There are some religions, some extremists, and some diet "specialists" that have been teaching that certain foods are forbidden or not recommended. Well, consider 1 Timothy 4:3-5, "……and commanding to abstain from foods which God created to be received WITH THANKSGIVING by those who believe and know the truth, for every creature of God is good, and nothing is to be refused if it is received with thanksgiving; for it is sanctified by the word of God and prayer." (caps mine).

Now here is a thought: Keep decreeing through prayer before you eat for the food to be blessed for the 'good taste' and nourishment only for your body. Now this doesn't give you license to over eat. Proverbs 23: 21: "For the drunkard and the glutton will come to poverty."

JUDGE NOT, LEAST YE BE JUDGED

I added this topic, because it has mostly been misused, especially by those who don't KNOW Jesus. In Matt 7:1, "Judge not, that you be not judged," you have to know who Jesus is speaking to. This 'speech' starts in Chapter 5. He is speaking to the multitudes, where most don't know Him and His Word intimately yet. So in 7:1, He is saying (paraphrasing), "how can you judge when you still have the "speck" (of your own unforgiven sin) in your eye." I have experienced many times that many of those same ones trying to use Matt 7:1, are also the ones who have decided, along with "their associates", which sins are okay and which sins are the worst you can do on earth, like being 'for' Gay marriage, but adultery is so bad that it is unforgiveable.

"But he who is spiritual (true Christians) judges all things, yet he himself is rightly judged by no one. For who has known the mind of the Lord that he may instruct Him? But we (true Christians seeking Him) have the mind of Christ." (1 Corinthians 2:15, 16, parenthesis mine). In 1 Corinthians, 6:2 & 3, "Do you not know that the saints (true Christians) will judge the world? And if the world will be judged by you, are you unworthy to judge the smallest matters? Do you not know that we shall judge the angels? How much more things that pertain to this life?" What is extremely important is for the Christian worker's simple relationship with Jesus Christ to be strong and GROWING. Our usefulness to God depends on that, and that alone.

The calling of Christians is to expose sin (Ephesians 5:11), and to reveal Jesus Christ as savior. Consequently, we cannot always be charming and friendly, but must be willing to be stern to accomplish major surgery. We are sent by God to lift up Jesus, do His 'works and greater works', not to give wonderfully beautiful speeches, which is what multitudes of 'Christians' would rather hear. That is why I have experienced many churches filled, so as to make people feel good, maybe with a little good "Word from the Bible", but even most of them have their mind on for the service to hurry and be over so they can go barbecue, or whatever. Granted, this is better than no church at all. So we must be willing to examine others as deeply as God has examined us. We must be sharply intent on sensing those scripture passages that will drive the truth home, and will not be afraid to apply them. This gets more bolder to do and more effective the more consistent you stay in the "seeking of getting to KNOW Jesus." But, be careful to use "Judge not, lest you be judged" on others, for it may be God working through another saint to "steer" you more in His direction.

GIVING

My topics in this book are not prioritized in order of importance. This subject, though, is one of the most important, yet the least used by most Christians. I have been tithing and giving offerings from the beginning in 1981, although my wife did not agree. She even convinced my children that I cared more for tithing than I did in spending the money for the family. They did not understand then, and probably still don't, that you tithe and give offerings to TRUST GOD with your finances and know that He will look after all your "needs". And you're giving it to God. What the church does with it is between them and God. But those "needs" doesn't mean to buy expensive tennis shoes every couple months, because your 'skate board' son tears them up, as example. Too many parents these days are held hostage by their own kids to keep buying them things that are NOT necessary, like buying every new i-phone that comes out. And besides that, most of the kids are not doing any chores to "earn" it, and are probably not even making up their own beds. Now, I may not have handled these problems always perfectly right, but as head of the household, I trusted God with our finances. We never went hungry, run out of clothes to wear, and always had shelter, and could afford a MacDonald's hamburger here and there. Things did get better slowly but surely despite the negatives. The following is from one of the articles we covered in Sunday school at Jubilee Church:

"Jesus Christ said more about money than about any other single thing because, when it comes to a man's real nature, money is of first importance. Money is an exact index to a man's true character. All through scripture there is an intimate correlation between the development of a man's character and how he handles his money." Richard Halverson.

I have actually heard many different times and ways 'excuses' of why people won't give to the church. A common one is that they don't like that the pastor drives a Mercedes, or the pastor's wife has too much jewelry. Well, again, that is between them and God. I know though examples of where God rewards in "things" and wealth. He is rewarding those who are doing His Will, and He would rather you drive a Mercedes than an old pickup truck. Probably, that is what 'that' pastor started with, anyway. But the usual 'excuse' is because they have no faith, and/or are just not interested in following 'God's Way'.

In Matthew 19: 16-22, it basically refers to a rich man asking Jesus what to do to receive eternal life. Jesus knew what controlled the man, who said he had been 'good' all his life following the commandments, so Jesus said the man should sell all and give it to the poor. Well, the rich man went away in sorrow. Now Jesus knew that Judas would betray Him, and that man could have been one of the twelve disciples. Hence, trust God. Note: I was NOT thinking of this story when at the end of 2019, it was decided for me to sell my house, car, and household goods and furniture. When God led me to Mike Brawan in 2017, He knew in advance that I would follow His 'still silent voice' to sell and move to Kenya. So in Kenya, we had done some great things despite the corona fear with restrictions. God told me a while back in the USA to write a book, but I didn't do it. But Mike told me during all the restrictions to write a book in May, 2020, so I wrote this book, even still being anxious to be more out and about with the people. So, I ended up doing the right thing the 'rich man' did not do. Praise be to God!

Now remember, "money is not the root of all evil", it is "the love of money that is the root of all evil". (1 Timothy 6:10). Hence, drugs, prostitution, sex slaves, using young kids in forced labor, alcoholism, wrong kind of parties, gambling addiction, power hunger, using welfare unjustly, abiding to corona restrictions (W.H.O., etc. paid countries to enforce), socialism, and even not tithing (just putting a dollar in the offering plate to 'feel' good), are all examples of the 'love' of money.

Tithe is considered 10% of your gross income. I have said this for years: that 10% would enable the 90% left over to go further than the 100% would have, especially if you are a 'cheerful giver'. 2 Corinthians 9: 6-8, "……..He who sows sparingly will also reap sparingly, and he who sows bountifully will also reap bountifully. So let each one give as he purposes in his heart, not grudgingly or of necessity; for God loves a cheerful giver. And God is able to make all grace abound toward you that you, always having all sufficiency in all things, may have an abundance for every good work." Wow, abundance for all the good works you do, and the more you give, in this manner, the more you receive. Now imagine, husbands and wives, how MUCH more you will 'realize' this with your owns eyes, IF YOU ARE BOTH IN AGREEMENT! You will not always 'see' the physical evidence as quick as you would like, but God has 'ways and timing' that is usually, beyond your "seeing' it. I have actually noticed several times that my bank account had more money than I thought, and I majored in a mathematics type degree.

I personally have studied from several wealthy pastors and evangelists. They ALL basically gave abundantly in the beginning while in various stages of poverty, and still do, and have great works of many kinds throughout the world. Plus, I have met some and knew the testimonies of many wealthy business men and women of God who gave liberally and thus have such huge business success to employ hundreds. These folks are also a major part of the taxes paid to the government. Don't get hung up in a few that pay less due to 'loop holes and international sources'. Now the liberalists have used a lot of those taxes to pay for free abortion, supporting immoral sexual activities, unrighteous welfare, free medical to illegals, and much more. But, depending who was president, many righteous things were done as well. But this is another huge subject maybe for another book.

In conclusion, God will test your heart many ways with money. Make sure you're not one "to have a hundred shoes, but only give a dollar in the offering plate". And make sure you GIVE abundantly as you are getting to know Jesus, and you will receive that 'knowing' readily and in abundance and be ready for promptings from Him at any time to give 'X' amount at any time for any 'cause'.

SOME WORTHY SHORT TOPICS

In the past one of the many churches I attended for a while in the search for the "right" church, was actually an adult Sunday school class that even had a couple pastors as 'students'. There were many discussions with lots of participation on whatever verses were being studied. One day there was a study on 2 Corinthians 12: 7-10. It was about Apostle Paul's "thorn in the flesh." This is where it was confirmed to me that so many Christians think that God either uses or causes sickness to test people. Excuse me, but that is horse crap! They say Jesus is using the "thorn" as a sickness to test Paul of how he will handle it, because Jesus said in response to Paul asking 3 times for God to get rid of the thorn from him, in verse 9: "My grace is sufficient for you...." as if Jesus is telling Paul, "don't worry, I will handle it when I am ready." Well, the true meaning is, "My Grace, Jesus in you, is sufficient for YOU to solve that problem, and for you to say, 'By the Authority of the Name of Jesus, thorn, be gone!"

I was reading a book where another mighty man of God was trying to listen to Jesus, who was in his presence, but there was a little ugly demon in between them that was creating too much havoc, so he could not hear Jesus very well. He wondered why Jesus didn't get rid of it, so finally he said, "Be gone in the Name of Jesus", and it left. Jesus then said, "I am glad you did that…..I could not." The man of God didn't understand, then Jesus said, "I gave you the Authority to do that." Remember since we are in heavenly places with Jesus (Ephesians 2:6), per Ephesians 1:21, "…are far above all principality and power and might, and DOMINION, and every name that is named….", whether it be demons, corona virus, cancer, and so much more.

Another one I heard from an atheist. When Adam fell in sin and hid from God in the Garden of Eden, and God asked "where are you?", why would God ask that if He IS God? Well, most Christians at any level should know the answer. Adam was hiding because, he knew he now had sin, and sin and God can't co-mingle. So God is asking pretty much "Where are you from now on?", and Adam and Eve were banished from Eden. There can be other teaching here concerning this subject.

Another short topic: Before the Cross and after the Cross: Before, Matthew 19:17, "….But if you want to enter into life, keep the commandments." See Jesus followed the Mosaic Law perfectly as a "man" on the earth. After, Acts 16:31, "….Believe on the Lord Jesus Christ, and you will be saved." Before, Mark 11:26, "But if you do not forgive, neither will your Father in heaven forgive your trespasses." After, Ephesians 4:32, "……forgiving one another, just as God in Christ also forgave you."

One more topic: Are you a Lukewarmer? When I was in Iraq we had about 30 drivers join us from the African country, Ghana. I became friends with them; some were Christians, some Muslims. After about

2 months, about 8 of them came to me complaining how the 'white' were treating them. After a couple minutes, I said, "No matter what country you go to, what your religion you are, what job you have, or what race you are, you will have your good, your bad, and your ugly!" You just can't reach out and change someone's heart very quickly. Then I pointed to one of them with a smile, and said, "See, he's your ugly one!" Well, they laughed, but they understood. I have referred to this story several times in discussing people in general.

But lately God revealed to me about Revelation 3:16 about Lukewarmers that I wrote about earlier. Lukewarmer takes the place of "ugly". This is where it says that God will "spit you out!" Wow, that's not good! So the main reason I'm writing this is because, in this world you are either the good, the bad, and or now the Lukewarmer, and like me, you have done a little 'back and forth' in your life. But as a whole, going through life, where is your heart? Too many think they are good, but according to the world's standards (grow up, get a good education, get a good job, work hard, etc.). The ones that are bad, just pick ANY excuse, and they will use it out of pride to make them 'look good'. And this world, under the dominion of Satan, loves the lukewarmer. Probably, the best example is to say they are Christian but support Gay marriage and/or abortion, or they vote for liberalists for their own agenda of wanting welfare, free medical, or free college. And because they are not trying to get to KNOW Jesus, they fall for 'persuasive' speakers that have 'hidden agendas' that are not good. But probably the worst about lukewarmers is their pride. They have to be right no matter how wrong they are. Example, to hide the idea that they just don't want to accept Jesus, there are hundreds of different things 'others' have said against Christianity, and they will use some of them as if it was their original ideas. Like the one about a preacher at that church down the street committed adultery so Christianity is wrong, and they "choose" not to believe in Jesus.

So please don't try to keep one foot in the 'good' direction and the other in the ungodly direction just to look good to your unrighteous friends. Go with God, and find new friends, maybe at the right church you will find if you look for it.

CHAPTER 6

KEYS TO HEALING

When I first started as a missionary with Impact Nations, they taught a "healing model", then they demonstrated it in the field. This is just a guideline, as there are some other different methods used by effective healers.....all, of course, using the Authority of the Name of Jesus. It is six steps:

1. Ask the person, "May I pray for you?"
2. Ask, "What do you want Jesus to do or ask what is the problem?" Have them be specific and not with a long list. If a malady in or on the body, ask where it is and what is it. Place your hand there (unless a lady's privates, if so, put her hand on it and you place your hand on top of hers). Listen to God a moment if there is anything He wants you to know or to say. It might be something like un-forgiveness in that person that needs to be addressed first.
3. Invite God's love, "thank you Father for loving (say the person's name)."
4. COMMAND by the Authority of the Name of Jesus for the 'malady', BE GONE!

5. Test it, if applicable. Sometimes you may have to repeat the process, as there may only be partial healing, and you want 100%.

It is critical here to EXPECT THE HEALING! Know it will happen! Check Acts 10:38, where, "God anointed Jesus....who went....healing ALL.....", not just some, not who deserved it, not just one 'type' of person.....but ALL. Remember Hebrews 11:1, where faith IS the substance of what is coming. The more you do this, the more you expect, and then the more you will SEE. I have discovered and read about all kinds of healing that all started with getting to KNOW Jesus, and getting up and going to DO something! It is the repetition of consistently reading, praying, and going and you gain that expectation.

Also, all along, know WHO Jesus is, and by knowing that you're doing "His works and greater works" that He wants of you (John 14:12). He loves to heal, not to test you. Now, in your affliction, before healing, yes, He wants to see HOW you handle it. He did not put the affliction on you! NO, it is not His Will for your sickness, nor are tornadoes, hurricanes, and earthquakes and such, "Acts of God!" Those are lies from the devil, but from the mouths of some, it can sound awfully right if you don't KNOW Jesus.

In the ones to be healed, look for their faith.........perceive 'their' expectations. Expect immediate healing, but sometimes just remember, "God's Ways and Thoughts are higher than ours," (Isaiah 55:8 & 9, paraphrased). God works through doctors and medicine sometimes, too. And the healing may not be visible till later. But KNOW they ARE healed. I was in the Philippines in 2018 as I wrote earlier. We were going 'hut to hut' praying and healing. One that I went to had a little girl looking real sad and sick with asthma. I prayed in the Name of Jesus for it to be gone. Nothing seemed to happen, and I had to go. Well, later in the center of that village we fed a lot of people, but had food left over. So we went back out 'hut to hut' to give to the ones who had not been there. That girl and her family had not been there, so I took some of that food to them. When I got there the little girl was jumping all over and laughing as she had been healed. Praise God! That was just one example out of several others.

HEAVENLY PARTICIPATION

Learn as you're getting to KNOW Jesus how to participate in heavenly activity here on earth. God is moving all the time. Be sensitive to try and keep up. Be aware and expect 'suddenlies', His sudden presence. Expect the Holy Spirit to prompt you to do, say, or write something. It might be just to say hi to someone. While I was in Kenya I was at a mall in Nakuru waiting on someone. A good looking blonde (yes, my eyes are still open as a widower) was about to walk pass me, so I said to her, "I don't see very many blondes here in Nakuru." Well, we talked a little. She told me her husband (Yeh, I was a little disappointed) had been a farmer for years there in Nakuru County. I told her I was a missionary, and mentioned some of the things we had been doing. Before we departed I told her to tell her husband, "Congratulations, for picking a good looking lady." The main point is I gave her a compliment and shared the good works being done in our ministry. Now what became of that is between her and God, because I don't know if there were any problems with her life. Maybe a seed was planted for them to go to a church, or maybe ours. I am meeting people all the time, and I am friendly, and maybe give them a compliment. Some of you reading this, maybe that is 'your' calling for now: meet people and make their day better, so they may do something righteous due to their improved attitude.

Just keep releasing the purposes of God by doing what seems to be right, whether it is healing someone, or just making their day better, or helping the poor, or helping an old lady cross the street, or a multitude of other righteous acts. "Whatever you release on earth is released in heaven, whatever you bind on earth is bound in heaven." (Matthew 16:19, paraphrased). He gives us the Authority of His Name, and He wants us to exercise it. Use it or lose it. Matthew 25:29 (parenthesis mine), "For to everyone who has (faithfulness) more will be given……but from him who does not have, even what he has will be taken away." All the aspects of that Authority is portrayed in many places in the Bible. A lot was covered in my 'prayers' chapter 3. You decree His Word for YOU!

The more you exercise your life in getting to KNOW Jesus, and at the same time to meet people's needs by praying that Authority in their life, God will guide you step by step where He wants you, and His assignments always comes with favor, but you will not always recognize that it was given. Ever come to an intersection where you were going to turn right, but 'something' told you to go left? And what you didn't know was that He prevented you being in a terrible car wreck, you heard about in the news later. There are so many things we have been 'saved from', or given something good we were not expecting, and much more. These are 'favors', and when you witness them, thank God. Remember during all that you experience, learn to control the tongue. Never forget, God delights in you laying 'His Hands' on people through your hands in Jesus Name.

CHAPTER 7

MIKE BRAWAN'S WORD FROM GOD

I asked Pastor Mike Brawan for an input for this book, because he is the reason I was in Kenya, as I have reflected several times in this book. But the below is just a very small part of how God engineered the development of Mike Brawan's ministry, with a very extensive and international Christian growth background, even some politics, and associations and works with heads of government, world evangelists, and establishing churches all over Kenya, and many other countries. And IT IS NOT OVER YET! So here's Mike:

> "Glory to God, this is Mike Brawan. I have seen the hunt for God in my life, so I am excited to be part of this great move of God with my friend, Rich Smith. He's done a lot of missionary work for us in Kenya by the Grace of our Lord Jesus Christ. How God connects people is extraordinary, and I wanted to add something concerning this book about, "People don't know what they don't know." Now what you don't know can be very dangerous, because the Bible says that "my people are destroyed for the lack of knowledge" (Hos 4:6). The truth is

the things you don't know, besides being dangerous, they can also kill you faster. That's why Jesus said, "You shall know the truth, and the truth will set you free" (John 8:32). Knowing the truth is the ability to search for what you don't know yet, if you have the desire to look for it. God gave me an opportunity to know the truth, and that truth is nothing else but Jesus. One of the first things God taught to me, which Rich put this in the 'Preface', I have been living by all this time of doing God's Work. It is in the first verse of the Bible, Genesis 1:1, "In the beginning God......" So I kept Him in the 'beginning' of all I have done. I discovered that He gives you the knowledge as you go along, and things start unfolding by themselves.

I came from a very poor family. We were so poor that the poor people called 'us' poor. During that time I lost my parents, and it was like everything was gone. I never had any vision of why I was born, and I learned later that the Bible says, "where there is no vision, my people perish" (Prov 29:18, KJV). So people perish, because they don't have the wisdom to see who they are, and that when your destiny is locked, you start living a meaningless life, and that's why many people give up on life. They don't see the reason of living. I had lost my life, and gave up completely. I had no reason to live until I received the truth. I will never forget the very day when I went to a meeting with my friend Amos to hear the word of God. But I was going to that meeting to cause trouble, because when you're 'mean', you also start hurting other people. This is how I had survived up to that time. But the Word of God declared that if I was the only person in the world, Christ would've STILL died for my sins. The only thing He wanted was for me to accept Him in my life, and to start a new life.

It has been many years since I started pursuing His knowledge, and to know His purpose for my life. That knowledge gave me the ability to seek, which caused God to open doors that has connected me to be all over the world. By my own, I couldn't have done anything. These amazing doors that opened broke the power of poverty, sickness, death, and all the curses in my life, because they were dealt with by the Cross of Jesus. So there is power in the understanding and knowing that all that has been paid for. Many people walk around without knowing that their life has already been secured by the virtue of understanding this truth. It was through this knowledge I discovered that I had a 'calling' on my life to give hope to this hopeless world, and how I could fulfill this was by knowing the Word of God. Also, I connected myself with some people who have seen far more than I, and as you see me far above where I was, it is because I'm standing on those people's shoulders.

Having knowledge, you become teachable and humble. Remember that there is no humiliation this way. Life is a choice, and that's why the Bible says, "Behold, I lay before you death and life" (Deut 30:15,paraphrased), but the choice is yours, so I chose life through the knowledge of the Word of God. That's why people who think they're clever, steer people in the wrong direction. That's why it is important to not just think about their words, but walk towards knowledge. There is always a price to pay to steadily do this 'seeking', but it is the opportunity to grow. The biggest room in this world is the room of improvements, where anyone can change the wrong destiny they were on. So you have to work on getting on the right destiny with the right knowledge. This creates results that good things start taking place in your life that would have never happened, because of the strength of the Bible.

All of us have equal opportunity, irrespective of how you were born, where you were born, or the color of your skin or nationality. So all the advantages that people are born with is not how they came into this world, but how they live their life with the equal opportunity to choose. You lose that which is rightfully yours. In not knowing your destiny, even when you arrive, you don't know you have arrived. So before you start the journey, you have to declare your destination, and that's the power of knowledge, and that's why Christ came to give us knowledge, the greatest gift that man can have. It 'connects in order for you to collect.' If you are not connected you will always be corrected, with no collection.

With the power of knowledge, it will help you discern the right people that you can work with. And that's how I came to know my friend, Rich Smith, and many other friends that I have spent a lot of time with. We are changing the world by reaching a multitude of people to rescue their life, and let them know, 'it is not over until it is over.' Shalom, Shalom."

CONCLUSION

This book has provided some of my experiences, practices, what I have learned, prayers used, sample writings in the past, excerpts from 2 mighty men of God, and much more in the process of getting to KNOW Jesus. I am still doing that, but at the higher level God has brought me, especially in Kenya doing the 'works of Jesus and greater works.' And praise God even higher levels are coming as Jesus tarries to come and "take us up." I am just at the 'tip of the iceberg' in my zeal to want to KNOW Jesus. See, I have eternity with Him to get to KNOW more, and discover what He has for me to do and from whatever parts of the universe He sends me!

So the purpose of this book for you, I pray, is that you would develop the same or even higher zeal to "want to KNOW what you still don't know" about Jesus. Keep in mind of these end days of some persecution, so brace yourself and endure till the end. And during your journey, remember Isaiah 40:31, "But those who wait on the Lord shall renew their strength; they shall mount up with wings like eagles, they shall run and not be weary, they shall walk and not faint." In other words, DON'T QUIT!!

"Father in heaven, this book is for YOU to get all the glory for all the people's total SALVATION received and/or for their commitments to endeavor to get to KNOW YOU!

In Jesus Name, Amen! SO BE IT!"

www.ingramcontent.com/pod-product-compliance
Lightning Source LLC
Chambersburg PA
CBHW030347100526
44592CB00010B/864